RECONCILING YOGAS

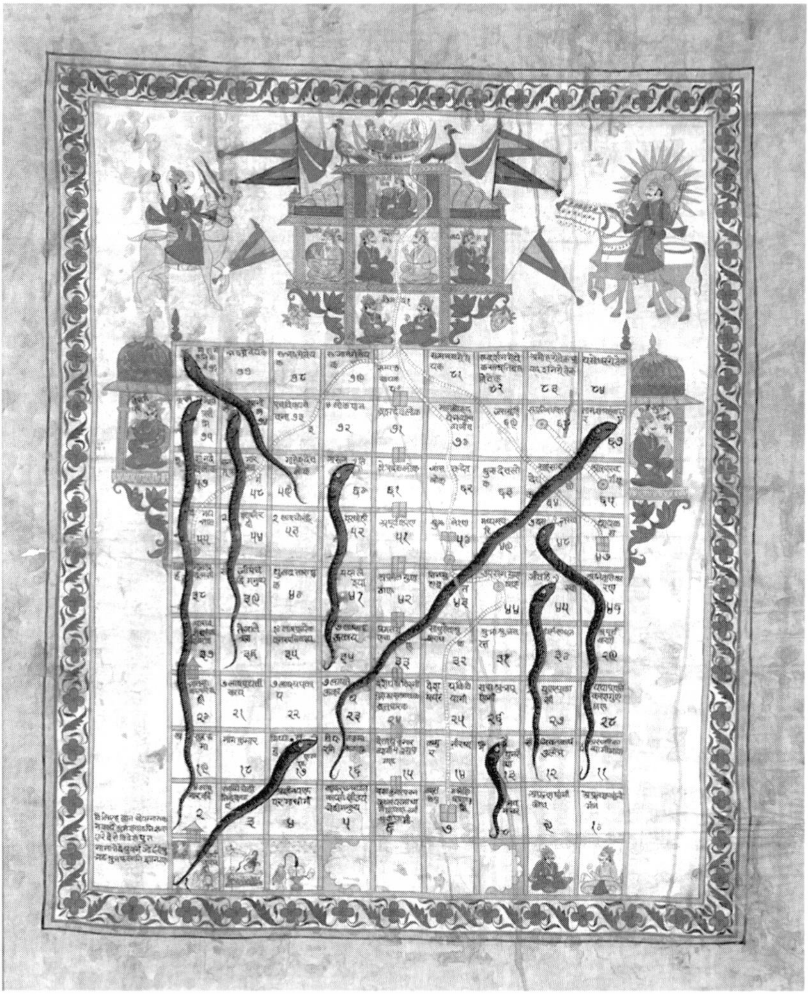

Eighteenth century Gyanbazi from Rajasthan.
Courtesy of Narendra and Rita Parson, Villa Park, California.

RECONCILING YOGAS

Haribhadra's Collection of Views on Yoga

Christopher Key Chapple

With a new translation of
Haribhadra's *Yogadṛṣṭisamuccaya*

by Christopher Key Chapple and John Thomas Casey

STATE UNIVERSITY OF NEW YORK PRESS

Published by
State University of New York Press
Albany

Printed in the United States of America

For information, address
State University of New York Press
90 State Street, Suite 700, Albany, NY 12207

Production, Laurie Searl
Marketing, Jennifer Giovani

Library of Congress Cataloging-in-Publication Data

Chapple, Christopher Key, 1954–
Reconciling yogas : Haribhadra's collection of views on yoga / Christopher Key Chapple ; with a new translation of Haribhadra's Yogadṛṣṭisamuccaya / by Christopher Key Chapple and John Thomas Casey.
p. cm.
Includes bibliographical references and index.
ISBN 0-7914-5899-7 (alk. paper)—ISBN 0-7914-5900-4 (pbk. : alk. paper)
1. Haribhadrasūri, 700–770. Yogadṛṣṭisamuccaya. 2. Yoga (Jainism)—Early works to 1800. I. Haribhadrasuri, 700–770. Yogadrstisamuccaya. English. II. Casey, John Thomas. III. Title.

BL1375.H37C43 2003
181'.044—dc21 2003042560

10 9 8 7 6 5 4 3 2 1

to

Maureen Shannon-Chapple

Contents

Preface

Haribhadra combines two primary concerns that have sustained and propelled me as a theologian and Yoga practitioner: respect for a plurality of perspectives and respect for personhood. During my very first class on the *Bhagavad Gītā*, which was conducted by members of the International Society of Krishna Consciousness at the State University of New York at Buffalo, I was concerned and a bit put off by the lecturers' insistence on Lord Krishna's status as the only true transcendent reality. The edge was finally taken off when one of the class leaders took to greeting me with Hari Oṃ, rather than Hare Krishna. Shortly thereafter, when I became affiliated with Yoga Anand Ashram in Amityville, New York, no deity image could be found: only a solitary flame, symbolic of the light and enlightenment to be revealed through the practice of Yoga.

Since that time, I have studied and learned about Christianity from Christians, Judaism from Jews, Islam from Muslims, Sikhism from Sikhs, Buddhism from Buddhists, and so forth. However, at the same time, I have learned about Vedānta from Christians, Judaism from secular scholars, and Pure Land Buddhism from a Catholic priest. Our circle of friends and acquaintances in Los Angeles includes overlapping communities of Yoga practitioners from a variety of traditions: Sikh, Kashmir Śaivite, Advaita Vedānta, Haṭha, and Raja, among others. Our world also includes Catholic priests and nuns, practicing Jews, and family members of various religious persuasions, including Sufis, Buddhists, Protestants, Catholics, and born-again Christians. Furthermore, to be situated within this amazing and wonderful amalgam of worldviews is not at all peculiar, at least in the part of the world that we inhabit. Our immediate neighbors to the left are members of Soka Gakkai, a Japanese Buddhist sect; on the right, our neighbors are Jewish; the young man who renovated our house, whose mother grew up here, is an American Sikh; and one long-time devotee of the Hare Krishna movement grew up in the house across the street.

Philosophically, how can we comprehend the world that has evolved into its present pluralistic shape? The religious landscape has become complex in ways that have been explored most recently by the Pluralism Project at Harvard University and earlier in the studies of American religious diversity by Robert Ellwood of the University of Southern California. One need not be a trained scholar to notice the many mosques and Hindu temples that have joined the ranks of mainline Protestant and Catholic churches and Jewish synagogues that can be found in virtually every American city. But my concern here is more than sociological; it extends to a concern for the development of intercultural understanding. Religions, for millennia, have been a source of individual and group identity that has created both a sense of belonging and a sense of otherness. We are all well acquainted with the violent legacy of religion, which stems from the tendency by religions to make non-coreligionists the "other" and sometimes even to construe the other as being less than human. We need only reflect on the many religious wars fought in times past and the wrenching violence that persists in Ireland, the Middle East, Sri Lanka, and elsewhere. In other, and, to my thinking, more auspicious situations, religion has become a tool not only for self-identity but for understanding and accepting the views of others.

The founders of the United States guaranteed religious freedom for all citizens. In our century, Martin Luther King Jr. and Mahatma Gandhi used Christian and Hindu ideas to forge more open, tolerant societies. Farther back in history, Wang Yang Ming integrated aspects of Confucianism, Taoism, and Buddhism to foster religious and social harmony in China. Thomas Aquinas learned of Greek scholasticism from the Muslims. Akbar synthesized Islam with Hinduism, Buddhism, and Christianity to proclaim a new, all-inclusive state religion, albeit a short-lived one. Guru Nanak, inspired by the poet, Kabir, moved beyond the boundaries of Islam and Hinduism to create Sikhism, and, at an earlier time in India, Jaina philosopher Haribhadra attempted to engage the key ideas of various traditions within the unifying theme of spiritual liberation. His concern to be fair to the views of others while maintaining one's own religious commitment and integrity led me to explore his *Yogadṛṣṭisamuccaya*, a text that exemplifies his method of promoting self-discovery within the parameters of one's tradition without utterly condemning the firmly held beliefs of others. In many ways, this book has emerged from an exploration of models of tolerance in light of plural and sometimes competing perspectives.

The other major concern that brought me to this study of the *Yogadṛṣṭisamuccaya* can best be described as respect for personhood. In my two decades of teaching at the university level, I have encountered students who have been, in some way or another, abused by religious authority. Most specifically, women have told me, sometimes in tears and sometimes with a sad, cynical worldliness, that they have been part of a "secret inner circle," granting sexual favors to an otherwise personally disinterested religious teacher or priest. This problem, which has been widely discussed in the popular journals of both Yoga and Buddhism in America and recently highlighted as a problem within Christian churches, crystallized for me in particular when Fred Lenz, a former fellow student at the State University of New York at Stony Brook, committed suicide in 1998. A horrific story came to light about how Fred, who had been a disciple of a New York-based Hindu teacher, used his flamboyant interpretation of meditation to gather a huge number of followers, amass millions of dollars, and sleep with hundreds of women. Ultimately, he fell into a deep depression and schemed not only to take his own life but convinced a young woman who had once been a close follower to accompany him in a double suicide. She survived, though he drowned off the dock of his estate on Conscience Bay, not far from Stony Brook.[1] Needless to say, Fred violated nearly every religious precept possible, including the foundational disciplines of his self-espoused Yoga. He lost his sense of respect for himself and the ability to see other persons as being worthy of respect.

Out of concern for those who might be lured to follow a teacher with dubious morals or credentials, I find Haribhadra's

Yogadṛṣṭisamuccaya a useful and instructive text on the importance of maintaining a moral compass on the spiritual quest. Haribhadra grappled with his own arrogance and developed a philosophy of tolerance and compassion. As we will see, the text describes the various temptations of power and enjoyment that one might encounter on the Yoga path and advises holding true to the principle of nonviolence in all of one's endeavors.

I am grateful to several people who helped in the development of this book. They include Nathmal Tatia, Douglas Renfew Brooks, Hartmut Scharfe, John Cort, Paul Dundas, Phyllis Granoff, Yajneshwar and Sunanda Shastri, Krishnan Chordia, Arindam Chakrabarti, Alex Wayman, Kristi Wiley, Olle Qvarnstrom, Samanis Charitra and Sharda Pragya, Pandit Dhiraj Lal Mehta, Pravin L. Shah, and especially my translation collaborator, John Casey. Earlier versions of select portions of this work appeared in John Cort's edited volume, *Open Boundaries*, Georg Feuerstein's *The Yoga Tradition*, and the volume edited by N. K. Wagle and Olle Qvarnstrom, *Approaches to Jaina Studies*. Dr. Yajneshwar Shastri of Gujarat University read carefully through the manuscript and made important suggestions regarding the translation, which, as he has noted, "conveys the essence of the verses rather than providing a word by word translation." Michael Bennett, Nicole de Picciotto, Virginia Huynh, Antonio Miranda, Marty McGee, Julie Chapple, and Emma Chapple were very helpful with the preparation of the manuscript. I am also grateful to my wife, Maureen Shannon-Chapple, to whom this book is dedicated, who carefully read through the manuscript and provided numerous corrections and suggestions.

CHAPTER ONE

The Life Story of Haribhadra

Haribhadra lived in India during a time of great philosophical diversity. The aftermath of the post-Gupta, pre-Islamic era witnessed a proliferation of Purāṇas, the flowering of Śaiva and Vaiṣṇava philosophy, early phases of the *bhakti* devotional movement in the south, the dawn of Tantra with a correlating emphasis on goddess worship, and the ongoing observance of the Vedic sacrificial system. Buddhism and Yoga were both strong presences within India and offered the most direct competition to Jainism, in that all three systems share an emphasis on self-effort in the quest toward spiritual uplift and liberation. In this book we will explore one particular text, the *Yogadṛṣṭisamuccaya*, that highlights Haribhadra's response to this complex religious landscape.

Haribhadra, according to one account, was the son of Śankarabhaṭṭa and his wife, Gaṅgā, born into the Brahmin caste. He lived either in Brahmapurī or in Citrakūṭa, which is "identified with Chittor, the capital of Mewar in Rajasthan."[1] He eventually became a Jaina monk of the Vidyādhara gaccha, headed by Jinabhaṭa, and he wandered throughout Western India as a member of the Śvetāmbara order.

This brings us to the question: when did Haribhadra live? Traditionally, Jainas have placed his dates from 459 to 529 C.E., which fits within the post-Gupta, pre-Islamic time frame. However, in 1919, Muni Jinavijayaji, a Jaina monk and scholar, published an extensive critique of these dates, noting that Haribhadra had quoted prominent authors who flourished after his supposed dates. As a result of this essay, Jaina and Western scholars alike have accepted later dates for Haribhadra, also known as Haribhadrasūri, from 700 to 770 of the Common Era. However, R. Williams contends that, in fact, some of the texts attributed to Haribhadra could have been written in the sixth century and suggests that there were two Haribhadras, with the eighth-century Haribhadra, whom he calls Yākinī-putra, imitating the style of an earlier master.[2] Most scholars agree with the assessment that Haribhadra lived during the eighth century rather than the sixth, and, although it cannot be denied that various people wrote under the name "Haribhadra," the consensus appears to favor a single Jaina Śvetāmbara author being responsible for at least most of the works attributed to him.[3] Due to its discussion of Tantra, it seems that the *Yogadṛṣṭisamuccaya* was written in the eighth century and, if one maintains the theory of two Haribhadras, would have been composed by Haribhadra Yākinī-putra, whose name in fact appears on the colophon. A third Haribhadra lived in the twelfth century and wrote a commentary on Umāsvāti's *Praṣamaratiprakaraṇa*.[4]

Hemacandra's *Yogaśāstra* (twelfth century) seems informed by Haribhadra's Yoga texts, and Yaśovijaya (seventeenth century) summarized and expressed renewed interest in Haribhadra's works, particularly on Yoga. His writings continue to be well known in the Śvetāmbara Jaina community.

Several traditional authors recorded legendary tales about the life, adventures, misadventures, and work of this prodigious scholar. Phyllis Granoff has summarized the primary stories about or related to Haribhadra, drawing from a variety of works that begin to appear in the twelfth century, including Bhadreśvara's *Kahāvali*, Sarvarājamuni's commentary on Jinadatta's *Gaṇadharārdhaśataka*, Prabhācandra's *Kathākośa* (1077 C.E.), a collection of stories known as the *Purātanaprabandhasaçgraha*, the *Prabhāvakacarita*, also attributed to a scholar known as Prabhācandra, but at a later date (1277 C.E.), and Rājaśekarasūri's *Prabandhakośa* (1349 C.E.) In these stories, two primary themes remain constant: Haribhadra's conversion to Jainism and his conflict with the Buddhists.

The first set of stories provides a biographical narrative. In his early years, Haribhadra, a member of the Brahmin caste, achieved a great degree of learning. He became quite arrogant about his academic accomplishments and tied a golden plate around his belly to prevent it from bursting from the weight of all his knowledge. In another version, he also carries a "twig from the jambu tree to show to all that there was no one his equal in all of Jambudvīpa, that is, in all the civilized world. He also carried a spade, a net, and a ladder in his desire to seek out creatures living in the earth, in water, and in the ether in order to defeat them with his great learning."[5]

Thinking he had learned all that could be known, he proclaimed that if anyone could tell him something new, he would devote his life to the pursuit of it. It so happened that he overheard a Jaina nun, Yākinī, reciting a verse he could not understand. Having been humiliated, he turned first to her and then to her teacher, Jinadatta, for instruction in the Jaina faith, which he then embraced. After a period of study, he was granted the title "Sūri," or teacher, and he began to promulgate Jainism. In several of his treatises, the colophon or final verse describes him as Yākinī-putra, or Yākinī's son, indicating the influence of this Jaina nun on his life and thought.

The second set of stories includes a dramatic and grisly tale of espionage, murder, and revenge. The *Prabhāvakacarita* of Prabhācandra (1277 C.E.) and the *Prabandhakośa* of Rājaśekharasūri (1349 C.E.) narrate the tragic story of two brothers, Haṃsa and Paramahaṃsa, who are both nephews and students of Haribhadra.[6] They go to Mahābodhi to learn about the teachings of the Buddha. The brothers are exposed as spies after uttering an invocation to the Jina when awakened by suspicious Buddhists in the middle of the night. They use umbrellas to float down out of the monastery. Buddhist soldiers catch and kill Haṃsa. Paramahaṃsa takes refuge with King Sūrapāla,[7] who proposes a debate between Paramahaṃsa and the Buddhists. The goddess, Tārā, secretly assists the Buddhists. The Jaina goddess, Ambā, advises Paramahaṃsa about how to trick Tārā by asking her to repeat what she had said the prior day, an impossibility for the gods, who are unable to keep track of time. Though Paramahaṃsa has won, because the Buddhists cheated, they still clearly intend to kill him. He hides as a laborer who washes clothes and then escapes to rejoin his uncle. As he tells the story to Haribhadra,

Paramahaṃsa dies from the grief that he suffers due to the death of his brother. Haribhadra is outraged. King Sūrapāla arranges a debate between Haribhadra and the Buddhists. One by one, the Buddhists are defeated and sent to their deaths in boiling oil as arranged by the king. Out of great remorse for the killing of so many monks, Haribhadra then composes his many religious treatises; according to Rajaśekhara Sūri, each of the 1,440 texts that Haribhadra wrote served as expiation for the 1,440 Buddhists who died.

The writings of Haribhadra reflect the conversion story and the story of his nephews in two possible ways. The story of his conversion from Brahmanism to Jainism makes sense in terms of his deep knowledge of Hinduism and the vehemence with which he discusses certain aspects of his former faith. He repeatedly criticizes in particular Vedic sacrifice and Tantric styles of worship. He also ridicules the worship of Krishna, declaring that because of his duplicity in the Mahābhārata war, Krishna resides in Hell. In his philosophical writings, he provides a standard Jaina critique of Upaniṣadic monism, which will be examined in a later chapter. This attitude of disdain toward Hinduism would make sense in light of the zeal often shown by a convert to a new faith, and it also reflects his intimate familiarity with the philosophy and stories of both the Brahmanical sacrificial tradition and the Kṣatriya epic tradition of Hinduism.

Although the story of the death of his two nephews is shrouded in several layers of historical ambiguity (see notes six and seven), it does provide some psychological texture to explain Haribhadra's motivation for writing so many texts and for being particularly solicitous of the Buddhists. By Haribhadra's time, Buddhism had lost its grip on the public and royal life of India. Many of the Buddha's ideas had been absorbed into the religious language of Hinduism, and in some accounts, Buddha was regarded as no more than an incarnation of Viṣṇu. Although many ideas of Jainism, particularly the emphasis on the five vows (nonviolence, truthfulness, not stealing, sexual restraint, and nonpossession), and the philosophy of karma had been similarly absorbed, primarily into the Yoga schools, Jainism remained distinct from Hinduism and survived, whereas Buddhism disappeared.[8] Although Haribhadra criticizes some of the aspects of

Buddhist philosophy (most notably the concept of momentariness, which will be discussed in a later chapter), he, in several texts, applauds the Buddhists, especially for their ideal of the Bodhisattva, the accomplished Buddhist who postpones his or her own enlightenment in order to help others.

THE WRITINGS OF HARIBHADRA

Even if Haribhadra did not write 1,440 treatises, he was prolific. H. R. Kapadia attributed eighty-seven works to Haribhadra,[9] including several very short pieces. More conservatively, Muni Jinavijaya lists twenty-six Haribhadra texts. Sukh Lal Sanghavi affirms Haribhadra's authorship of forty-seven texts and lists an additional twenty-six titles improbably attributed to Haribhadra.[10] He wrote in Prakrit, the language generally used by Jaina scholars, and he was one of the early Jainas to write in Sanskrit, the language generally associated with Brahmins and Mahāyāna Buddhists.

Haribhadra's two major Prakrit texts are the *Samarāiccakahā*, which is a collection of moral fables in novel form, and the *Dhūrtākhyāna*, which provides a satirical critique of Hindu mythology. The story of Yaśodhara first appears in Haribhadra's *Samarāiccakahā* and was retold in Hariṣeṇa's *Bṛhatkathākośa*, a Sanskrit text written in 931, and later in Somadeva's *Yaśastilaka*, written in 959. The tale merits discussion, because it quintessentially conveys key aspects of Jaina doctrine: the sufferings of life from one birth to the next and the consequent search for liberation.

In this story, King Yaśodhara discovers his beloved principal wife committing adultery. The wife then poisons Yaśodhara and his mother, Candramatī, while they sacrifice a rooster made of flour to the local goddess. He is reborn as a peacock, and his mother is reborn as a dog. Both end up back in the court as pets of Yaśodhara's son, Yaśomati, who is now king. One day the peacock remembers his former life as king and again sees his former wife making love to the same man. The peacock tries to kill them both, but they wound him and get away. The dog (his former mother) sees the hurting peacock (her former son) and kills it. King Yaśomati, annoyed that his dice game has been disturbed, hits the dog (his former grandmother) and kills it.

Yaśodhara is then born as a mongoose to a blind female and a lame male, who are unable to care for him. He survives by eating snakes. His mother, reborn as a cobra, engages him in battle. A hyena interrupts their fight and kills them both. Yaśodhara is reborn as a fish; his mother is reborn as a crocodile, which is later reborn as a she-goat. The fish lives a while longer and then is caught and fed to his former wife, Queen Amṛtamatī, as a result of his former action or karma. He next takes birth as a goat and impregnates his former mother. At the moment of his climax, he is gored by another goat and killed, but he enters her womb as his own son. His former son, King Yaśomati, hunts and kills the goat that had once been his grandmother, but he releases and spares the baby goat (his father) from her womb. One day, Yaśomati plans a big sacrifice to the goddess, Kātyāyanī, involving the killing of twenty buffaloes. His mother (Yaśodhara's former wife) does not want to eat buffalo meat that day and asks for goat instead. The cook slices some of the backside of the goat, who was once Yaśodhara. His former mother had been reborn as a buffalo; both were roasted by the cooks of the court.

The last phase of their tale finds both reborn as chickens in a tribal village. Their untouchable keeper, Caṇḍakarmā, begins to learn about Yoga and meditation. A yogi teaches him about the foundations of Jainism and, during the course of their discussions, tells Caṇḍakarmā about the past lives of the two chickens and how their adherence to princely dharma caused them repeated suffering. The chickens, having learned of their past tribulations, decide to accept the precepts of Jainism. In their joy, they utter a crowing sound. At that moment, Yaśodhara's son, Yaśomati, boasts to his wife that he could kill both chickens with a single arrow. Upon their death, Yaśodhara and his mother enter the womb of Yaśomati's wife and are eventually reborn as twins. Yaśomati continues his cruel ways of hunting until one day he encounters a Jaina sage, whom he urges his hounds to kill. They refuse, and the king has a change of heart. He spares the sage, who in turn tells him the amazing tale of the twin children (Yaśomati's father and grandmother) and how their misadventures were prompted by the sacrifice of a rooster made of flour. The king embraces the Jaina faith. The twins grow up to be great renouncers. They later convince an entire kingdom to give up animal sacrifice and eventually, having taken their final monastic vows, they fast to death and attain a heavenly state, further inspiring their kingdom to widely embrace Jaina practices. The moral of the story, included in the final verses, states: "He who carelessly effects the killing of one living being will wander aimlessly on the earth through many a rebirth."[11]

Haribhadra's more philosophical texts were written in Sanskrit. In the *Anekāntajayapatākā* and the *Śāstravārtāsamuccaya,* Haribhadra demonstrates his wide grasp of numerous sects of both Hinduism and Buddhism. These texts indicate his interest in developing "doxographies" or catalogues that summarize the philosophical positions of others. Phyllis Granoff observes:

> Even at his most disputatious, in a text like the *Śāstravārtāsamuccaya*, which is written with the sole intent of refuting rival doctrines, Haribhadra makes clear at the very onset of the text that his motives are not to stir up hatred and dissent, but to enlighten his readers and bring them the benefits of ultimate spiritual peace. Haribhadra's respect for the Buddha is unmistakable when he calls him *mahāmuni*, "the great sage" and one is left with the general impression that Haribhadra's respect for his Buddhist opponents is unchanged by his philosophical differences with them on specific points.[12]

Unlike Buddhist and Vedanta summaries, which sometimes tend to exaggerate or misrepresent the positions of rival schools, Haribhadra has proven to be a highly reliable source for learning about the authentic teachings that were promulgated in post-Gupta India. For instance, his *Saḍdarśanasamuccaya*, a brief text of eighty-seven verses, is used even today in India and in the United States as a textbook for summarizing the major strands of Indian thought.[13] His *Aṣṭakaprakaraṇa* lists eight qualities that can be universally applied to the faithful of any tradition: nonviolence, truth, honesty, chastity, detachment, reverence for a teacher, the act of fasting, and knowledge. Paul Dundas has noted that:

> The remarkable scholar Sukhalal Sanghvi, who overcame the handicap of blindness, contracted very early

> in life to become one of the most incisive of recent interpreters of Jain philosophy, described Haribhadra in a tribute as a *samadarshi*, "viewing everything on the same level," and his eminence derives not just from the breadth of his intellectual command but from his willingness to articulate more clearly than any of his predecessors the full implications of Jainism's main claim to fame among Indian philosophical systems, the many-pointed doctrine.[14]

Through his extensive writings, Haribhadra demonstrates his commitment to understand and respect the views of others while maintaining his commitment to the core Jaina beliefs in nonviolence and the need to purify oneself of the influences of karma.

RESPECTING THE VIEWS OF OTHERS IN THE *YOGADṚṢṬISAMUCCAYA*

Haribhadra's concern for respecting the views of all people of good faith can be seen throughout the *Yogadṛṣṭisamuccaya* (*YDS*), the shorter of Haribhadra's two Sanskrit texts on Yoga. First of all, he always refers to good action in the most general terms, recommending that people follow the holy books (*śāstras*) but without specifying which books ought to be followed. He emphasizes that although one may attain omniscience (*sarvajña*), each person will remain different and distinct (*YDS* 103). The content of experience is not shared; rather, the contentlessness of purity, which cannot be quantified in any way, is the only common element within the experience of liberation or omniscience. He uses the metaphor of a king's servants: "Just as a king has many dependents, divided according to whether they are near or far, etc., nonetheless, all of them are his servants" (*YDS* 107). He states that even though they may have different names, the core, purified essence of the liberated ones remains constant (*YDS* 108). Although acknowledging differences among those who have achieved liberation, nonetheless he regards all of them to be grounded in a common truth.

In a later section of the text (*YDS* 129–52), Haribhadra emphasizes that truth, though expressed differently, is not essentially different. Making references to Śaivites, Vedāntins, Yogins, and Buddhists, he states:

> "Eternal Śiva; Highest Brahman; Accomplished
> Soul, Suchness":
> With these words one refers to it,
> though the meaning is one
> in all the various forms. (*YDS* 130)

He goes on to state that this highest truth, by whatever name, frees one from rebirth (*YDS* 131). Demonstrating his commitment to a plurality of perspectives, Haribhadra comments that a variety of teachings is needed, because people need to hear things in their own way. Different seeds yield different plants; one cannot expect all things to be the same. He goes on to observe that:

> Perhaps the teaching is one
> but there are various people who hear it.
> On account of the inconceivable merit it bestows,
> it shines forth in various ways. (*YDS* 136)

This sentiment seems to be offered in atonement for the past arrogance that so characterized the Haribhadra of legend.

Haribhadra makes a plea for tolerance, writing that "various perspectives on conduct" can arise (*YDS* 138), but that these should not be criticized, as one cannot be apprised of all the circumstances (*YDS* 140). He advocates a stance of reconciliation and insists that it would be horribly improper to refute or revile well-intentioned people:

> Hence it is not proper
> to object to words of reconciliation.
> Refuting or reviling noble people, it seems,
> would be worse than cutting one's
> own tongue. (*YDS* 141)

He says that even if one disagrees with another person's ideas, one should always strive to be helpful to others. He criticizes the notion that logic alone can set one free, noting that:

With effort, even a position inferred
through the proper establishment of premises
may certainly be approached in another way,
being assailed by opponents. (*YDS* 145)

If the meaning of those things beyond the senses
could be known through a statement of reason,
then by now it would have been ascertained
by the scholars. (*YDS* 146)

In other words, thoughts alone cannot set one free; in contrast, the arrogance associated with logic and scholarship can be a great impediment to one's liberation. He says that liberation requires a loosening of attachment to all things (*dharmas*), including argumentation and logic.

Haribhadra concludes this section with an appeal to be kind and generous to all people. He writes that:

Even the slightest of pain to others
is to be avoided with great effort.
Along with this
one should strive to be helpful at all times. (*YDS* 150)

This verse echoes a recurrent theme found in Jaina texts. He then takes on a theme akin to the Bodhisattva ideal of Mahāyāna Buddhism:

Even in regard to those with excessive sin
who have been cast down by their own actions,
one should have compassion for those beings,
according to the logic of this highest *dharma*. (*YDS* 152)

According to the example set by Haribhadra, the task of the philosopher and of the Jaina is to extend compassion toward other living beings.

Haribhadra epitomized the Jaina commitment to noninterference with the life of others, as put forth by the doctrine of nonviolence. He was a convert to Jainism and most likely had a great deal of zeal, to the extent that he wrote scathing satires on the Hindu myths he knew so well, and perhaps he sent his own nephews to spy on the Buddhists.[15] If we follow the Haribhadra stories told centuries after his death, he seems to have learned from his youthful arrogance and possible violence and developed a philosophical approach that includes being somewhat open to the views of others. John Cort has suggested that the Jainas are not tolerant in the same way as the modern liberal secularists, and certainly Haribhadra unequivocally does not hedge his commitment to the core teachings of Jainism, even while competently presenting the views of others.[16] However, as Granoff and Dundas have noted, he exhibits a depth of friendliness to non-Jaina views. Granoff notes that: "Haribhadra exhibits a remarkable broad-mindedness in terms of doctrine; in many cases he states clearly that one should not reject a religious teaching if it is true, even if it is found in an opponent's writings; one should instead act with an open mind and be prepared to accept any religious tenet that is in conformity with logic and is correct."[17] Haribhadra's statements in the *Yogadṛṣṭisamuccaya* underscore his mission to understand the views of others in an attempt to clarify his own thinking and practice.

THE CONTEXT FOR HARIBHADRA'S STUDIES OF YOGA

Haribhadra's writings on the Yoga tradition provide an eighth-century analysis of Yoga from the Jaina perspective. They provide significant information on the practice of Yoga in post-Gupta India. They also shed light on philosophical aspects of the Jaina tradition and demonstrate the vitality of Jaina intellectual life during this period. The term *Yoga* is used widely in the religious traditions of India. Although generally associated with either the classical Yoga system of Patañjali (ca. 200 C.E.) or with the later Haṭha Yoga tradition, Yoga also is used as a generic description for religious practice in the *Bhagavad Gītā,* as well as in texts of both Buddhism and Jainism.

As Mircea Eliade and other historians of religion have noted, Yoga has roots deep in the protohistory of the Indian subcontinent. Indus Valley amulets from four or five millennia ago depict what appear to be early yogins. The *Ṛg Veda* refers to practitioners of exotic ascetic techniques, and by the time of the Upaniṣads, different forms of Yoga are mentioned in very explicit terms. By the time Patañjali composed his 195 aphorisms on Yoga, entitled the *Yoga Sūtras,* in the early centuries of the Common Era, a common definition for Yoga had been accepted: *citta vṛtti nirodha,* or stilling the fluctuations of the mind. Key to this definition is the term *nirodha,* a Buddhistic term alluding to the great restraint required to conquer the wandering mind.

By the time of Haribhadra, Yoga had gained prominence both as one of the six discrete schools of philosophical Brahmanism and as a practice followed by devotees of diverse religious paths. The *Bhagavad Gītā* reflects the diversity of Yoga, proclaiming several of its forms supreme: Karma Yoga, through which one is detached from the fruits of one's action; Jñāna Yoga, the insight meditation practiced by the learned; and Bhakti Yoga, devotion to one's chosen deity, which in the *Bhagavad Gītā* entails worship of Krishna. In addition to these sanctioned or recognized forms of Yoga, several Tantric schools were popular in the eighth century, including the Kaula school and various Śaivite cults.

Most scholarship on Yoga has focused on its Hindu manifestations, as summarized by Mircea Eliade, in his *Yoga: Immortality and Freedom,* and updated with research by Georg Feuerstein and many other scholars. Lengthy bibliographies have been published on Hindu Yoga. Also, scholarship on Buddhist forms of Yoga has been extensive and includes works by early Buddhologists such as Emile Senart and Louis de la Vallee Poussin and recent scholars, particularly of the Tibetan tradition, such as Jeffrey Hopkins and others.

While Jainism, which dates from perhaps as early as the eighth century B.C.E., makes a significant contribution to the Indian intellectual tradition, it has received far less attention from modern scholars than Hinduism and Jainism. Jaina philosophy and practice have had a profound influence on Indian history. The tradition is thoroughly atheistic in that it refutes any notion of a creator God or an external controlling force. It advances a theory of multiple life forms (*jīva*) that are trapped within thick coatings of karma. Liberation (*kevala*) is to be achieved by ridding oneself of karma through one's own effort. The earliest surviving Jaina text, the *Ācārāṅga Sūtra* (ca. 350 B.C.E.), describes the rigors of asceticism designed to reduce one's karma, which in

Jainism is described in terms of a physically real, colorful, sticky substance. The *Tattvārtha Sūtra* of Umāsvāti (ca. 400 C.E., as suggested by Yajneshwar Shastri)[18] provides a detailed description of stages of spiritual advancement (*guṇasthāna*) grounded in the observance of nonviolence (*ahiṃsā*).

The Jainas work at the dissolution of karma through a highly detailed sequence of spiritual and ethical disciplines and observances, the most familiar of which is the avoidance of violence through a strict vegetarian diet and the adoption of particular lifestyles and occupations that promote harmlessness. Ultimately, the Jaina path leads to a state of perfect solitude (*kevala*), in which each soul dwells, unfettered by any tinge of karma. These doctrines distinguish Jainism from Hinduism's emphasis on deity worship and monism, as well as from Buddhism's insistence on impermanence and emptiness.

Umāsvāti developed extensive descriptions of the Jaina cosmology, metaphysics, and systems of meditation that entail the extirpation of karma. The Buddhist Abhidharma schools offered similar assessments of the world and the human condition. All three systems, Jaina, Buddhist, and Brahmanical, borrowed key ideas from the Sāṃkhya system.[19] Haribhadra, aware of these earlier traditions and eager to bring them into discussion with the Jaina traditions of Yoga, developed four or five texts that pertain to the topic of Yoga.

Yoga traditions held a particular fascination for Haribhadra. In Yoga he saw a tradition that emphasized practice rather than theory. By exploring various Yoga schools and by reexamining his own Jaina faith within the categories of Yoga, he was able to develop a language of universality that respected his own commitment to the highest goal of Jainism (*ayoga kevala*) while at the same time allowed him to affirm similar goals in other traditions.

Haribhadra (or the two Haribhadras) wrote two Yoga texts in Sanskrit, the *Yogabindu* and the *Yogadṛṣṭisamuccaya*, and two Yoga texts in Prakrit, the *Yogaśataka* and the *Yogaviṃśikā*.[20] These books have been translated into English by K. K. Dixit and published through the L. D. Series at the L. D. Institute of Indology in Ahmedabad. Some scholars also mention the *Soḍaśakaprakaraṇa* as a Yoga text, though it appears to deal primarily with sixteen aspects of Jaina worship.[21]

This book will focus on the *Yogadṛṣṭisamuccaya*, with an investigation of its relationship to Patañjali's *Yoga Sūtra*, its discussion of Buddhist and Vedāntin styles of Yoga, its critique of Tantra, and its unique way of emphasizing core ideas of the Jaina tradition.

CHAPTER TWO

Haribhadra and Patañjali

The Yoga system of Patañjali provides the template upon which Haribhadra erects the *Yogadṛṣṭisamuccaya*. Patañjali's system, based on Sāṃkhya philosophy, incorporates several key Buddhist practices and aspects of Jaina philosophy. By the time of Haribhadra, it had gained broad respect for its ability to integrate a wide array of religious practices without allowing itself to be dismissed as ideological or dogmatic. Specifically, it treads a middle path when it comes to theology. Like classical Sāṃkhya, Buddhism, and Jainism, Yoga rejects the notion of a creator and a controller, unlike the more theistic schools of Hinduism. However, it does allow for the presence of a spiritual entity, referred to as Īśvara, defined as a "distinct consciousness (*puruṣa*), untouched by afflictions, actions, fruitions, or their residue" (*Yoga Sūtra* I:24, hereafter abbreviated as *YS*). This provides a model for the spiritual aspirant, whose discipline and spiritual path (*sādhana*) require the purging of afflicted karma (*kliṣṭa-karma*). Like Jainism, Yoga emphasizes the practice of nonviolence (*ahiṃsā*) and refers to karma in terms of different colors (*leśya* in Jainism).

THE *YOGA SŪTRA* OF PATAÑJALI

Patañjali divides his *Yoga Sūtra* into four parts or Pādas: Absorption (*Samādhi*), Practice (*Sādhana*), Powers (*Vibhūti*), and Aloneness (*Kaivalyam*). The first section begins with the classic definition of Yoga: "stilling of the mind's fluctuations (*citta-vṛtti-nirodha*)"

(*YS* I:2). It then catalogues the five forms of mental activity: cognition, error, imagination, sleep, and memory, noting that these can exist in afflicted or unafflicted states. For the bulk of this chapter, Patañjali lists techniques for overcoming afflictions, including practice and dispassion; concentration on thought, reflection, bliss, and ego; application of faith, energy, mindfulness, concentration, and wisdom (a well-known Buddhist practice); dedication to Īśvara through the chanting of Oṃ; single-mindedness; application of the Brahma-Vihāra,[1] another well-known Buddhist practice; control of breath; binding of the mind; sorrowless illumination; abandonment of attachment; reflection on auspicious dreams; or any meditation, as desired (*abhimata-dhyāna*). The last section of the first chapter outlines various states of concentration that lead ultimately to the dissolution of the seeds of karma (*nirbīja-samādhi*).

The second section of the *Yoga Sūtra* (*Sādhana*) outlines two systems of practices, describes the nature of karmic affliction, and summarizes the Sāṃkhya philosophical perspective that undergirds Yoga. The first system of Yoga, Kriya Yoga, is said to lead to absorption (*samādhi*) and consists of austerity (*tapas*), study (*svadhyāya*), and dedication to emulating the supreme spiritual entity, Īśvara (*īśvara-praṇidhāna*). Haribhadra will introduce his *Yogadṛṣṭisamuccaya* with a similar, though not parallel, threefold system, which will be discussed in a later chapter.

Patañjali then outlines the causes of affliction: ignorance, egotism, attraction, aversion, and the desire to continue living. These afflictions pervade the root of karmic conditioning; Yoga practices seek to diminish them. Summarizing the Sāṃkhya system, he points out that all activity lies in the realm of the three ever-changing qualities of manifest reality, the *guṇas* of illlumination (*sattva*), passion (*rajas*), and lethargy (*tamas*). These three comprise the seen; through Yoga one seeks to distance oneself from this realm and, through discriminative discernment (*viveka-khyāti*), establish oneself in the pure consciousness of the seer (*draṣṭṛ*).

To accomplish this, Patañjali outlines eight component practices of Yoga, the famous Eight Limbs (*aṣṭāṅga*). Most of the second section is taken up with defining and describing the first five of these eight. The first component, Discipline or Yama, includes five ethical precepts, equivalent to the five primary vows of the Jaina tradition: nonviolence (*ahiṃsā*), truthfulness (*satya*), not stealing (*asteya*), sexual restraint (*brahmacarya*), and nonpossession (*aparigraha*). The highest of these five is nonviolence, which, echoing themes from the Jaina tradition, Patañjali proclaims constitutes "the Great Vow (*mahāvratam*) when not limited by birth, place, time, or circumstance on all occasions" (*YS* II:31). The second component, the Observances or Niyama, includes purity, contentment, and the three facets of Kriya Yoga listed above: austerity, study, and dedication to Īśvara. Descriptions of the next three components complete the second chapter: postures (*āsana*), breath control (*prāṇāyāma*), and inwardness (*pratyāhāra*).

The third section (*Vibhūti Pāda*) begins with an exposition of the final three components of Eightfold Yoga: concentration (*dhāraṇā*), meditation (*dhyāna*), and absorption (*samādhi*). Patañjali refers to these as the "inner limbs" and describes their role in gaining mastery over the mind. Through the collective application of these in a process known as *saṃyama*, various powers arise: knowledge of past and future, enhanced language learning capabilities, understanding of past births, clairvoyance, invisibility, premonition of death, great strength, knowledge of inner esoteric physiology (*cakras*), intuition, radiance, lightness, mastery of the elements, perfection of the body, mastery over the sense organs, and mastery over the creative process. These powers in themselves do not constitute a definitive or even an elevated religious accomplishment. In fact, Patañjali warns that these can be distractions, a concept that Haribhadra reasserts in the *Yogadṛṣṭisamuccaya*. Only one power yields liberation: the ability to see the difference between the seen (*prakṛti*) and the seer (*puruṣa*), which occurs through the refinement of and ongoing involvement with illumination (*sattva*).

The fourth (*Kaivalyam*) section includes a further explanation of the Sāṃkhya metaphysical system, a discussion of karma that includes reference to the colors of karma, mentioned above, and further clarification of the idea of liberation, noting that in the state of virtuous absorption (*dharma megha samādhi*), all afflicted action ceases. All propensity for worldly manifestation and involvement comes to an end, grounding the Yoga practitioner in the power of higher awareness (*citi-śakti*).

This text of fewer than 200 aphorisms became the standard manual for spirituality throughout India by the early centuries of the Common Era. It was translated into Arabic by the Islamic scholar, Al Biruni, and today it has been translated scores of times into Western languages. For Haribhadra, explaining Jaina Yoga in terms of Patañjali's system provided a means to communicate the Jaina message to a broader audience, probably with an eye to converting others, and it also lent to the Jainas a context for placing their tradition, often derided as extremist, within the broader intellectual spheres of India. As we will see in the next chapter, it was not only Haribhadra who borrowed the eightfold schematic, but, as he notes, two others, a Buddhist and a Vedāntin, also developed systems similar to Patañjali to advance their own versions of the spiritual path.

In the next section of this chapter, we explore the structure and contents of the *Yogadṛṣṭisamuccaya*. This will be followed with an analysis of how Haribhadra aligned this text with the widely accepted gradation of Jaina spirituality into fourteen stages (*guṇasthāna*), which, as mentioned above, Haribhadra does with a very light touch.

THE *YOGADṚṢṬISAMUCCAYA*

In the *Yogadṛṣṭisamuccaya*, a Sanskrit text of 228 verses, Haribhadra examines and compares several different schools of Yoga. He aligns Patañjali's eightfold scheme with three others (including one of his own) and also measures each against the traditional Jaina fourteenfold path to liberation. In addition, he describes four different sects of Yogis current at his time and states emphatically that any Yogis who become involved with goddess worship or Tantra run the risk of making no spiritual advancement. While he is both descriptive and critical of the Buddhists' emphasis on impermanence and of Brahmanical monism, Haribhadra provides little detail regarding the actual practice of Yoga in light of traditional Jaina categories such as karma and *jīva*.

Some scholars have tended to emphasize the seeming liberality of Haribhadra's attitude toward non-Jaina traditions (cf. Granoff, Dundas). Haribhadra is widely credited with a search for and commitment to respecting the views of others. However, upon close examination, this approach is not consistently applied in the *Yogadṛṣṭisamuccaya.* On the one hand, he can be cited as providing a paradigmatic example of the Jaina philosophy of *anekānta* or "many-sidedness," an approach that acknowledges the complexity and perspectival nature of human thought. However, in actuality, he continually sets up his argument not so much to affirm the wisdom of the Buddhists or the Vedāntins as to demonstrate the incompleteness of these systems. Though he praises other views and states that all forms of Yoga lead to liberation, nonetheless, he does not stray from his insistence on the primary Jaina tenets: karma causes suffering, and yogic disciplines purify one of karma and, hence, alleviate suffering. His gentle way of asserting this most fundamental aspect of Yoga perhaps exhibits a form of tolerance of other views and may be seen as an extension of the fundamental Jaina precept of nonviolence (*ahiṃsā*). But in other instances, he is quite acerbic in lambasting those who do not conform to his views, such as the Kula Yogis and those who deny the inherent reality of suffering.

The *Yogadṛṣṭisamuccaya* is not divided into chapters, however, after a benedictory verse, similar to the second section of Patañjali's *Yoga Sūtra*, Haribhadra begins with a threefold analysis of styles of Yoga. He then provides an extended eightfold analysis of Yoga. In the middle of this discussion, he engages in a long discourse against what he considers "misguided" Yoga practices. He concludes with a sociological survey of Yoga schools, presumably active during his life, and an appeal to the reader, hoping that his work will help inspire purity of heart in regard to Yoga.

The text opens with a benediction, acknowledging a relationship between the Yoga concept of Iśvara and the Jina. In the first section (*YDS* 2–8), he describes a threefold Yoga: Wishful Yoga, Precept Yoga, and Effort Yoga. As we will see in a later chapter, these correlate to categories of the Tantra tradition that was gaining in popularity in Haribhadra's time. He describes these three phases as successive. The first indicates a desire to enter into the Yoga path. The second signals a willingness to live according to the mandates of religious texts. The third involves persistent resolve to change one's behavior and bring it into

TABLE 2.1
The Threefold and Eightfold Yogas of Haribhadra

Sāmarthya	Effort
Śāstra	Precept
Icchā	Wishful

	Patañjali
Parā Highest	Samādhi Absorption
Prabhā Radiant	Dhyāna Meditation
Kāntā Pleasing	Dhāraṇā Concentration
Sthirā Firm	Pratyāhāra Inwardness
Dīprā Shining	Prāṇāyāma Breath Control
Balā Power	Āsana Postures
Tārā Protector	Niyama Observances
Mitrā Friendly	Yama Disciplines

[Christopher Key Chapple]

accordance with the rigors of religious life. This also might correspond to the three types of Yoga practitioners mentioned in Patañjali's first chapter: the mild, middling, and intense (see *YS* I:17) and perhaps to the threefold Jaina practice of insight, knowledge, and practice (*darśana*, *jñāna*, and *cāritra*). It does not, however, seem to correlate to Patañjali's triad of austerity, study, and devotion (*tapas*, *svadhyāya*, and *īśvarapraṇidhāna*).

Haribhadra next presents a thumbnail sketch of Jaina Yoga (*YDS* 9–11). Alluding to the *Tattvārtha Sūtra*, he speaks of two levels of renunciation. The first involves the renunciation of dharma, not in the sense of the *Bhagavad Gītā*, where dharma refers to duty or law, but in the Buddhist sense, as used in the *Abhidharmakośa* and in the way dharma is referred to in Patañjali's *Yoga Sūtra*. Dharmas are constituent factors of reality, including physical objects that manifest in the elements, sensory processes, and one's emotional makeup. In the preliminary phases of Jaina Yoga, one purifies and releases the karma that has conditioned these dharmas. This ultimately leads to the state of *sayoga kevala*, a preliminary state of liberation attained in the thirteenth stage. One begins to accomplish the renunciation of dharmas in the eighth stage (*guṇasthāna*), which will be explained below. The final renunciation, which occurs in the fourteenth stage, entails renouncing the connection itself that holds a person within the physical body. At this stage, one abandons the connection (*yoga*, here used as a technical term) with the karmas of sensation, life span, name, and caste. This final state, which occurs at the point of death, releases one from rebirth, allowing one to dwell in eternal energy, consciousness, and bliss. Though this summary of Jaina Yoga comprises only three verses, it alludes to the broader theories of Jaina karma theory and indicates the approach to Patañjala Yoga to be taken by Haribhadra, which will be explained more fully below.

In the next eight verses (*YDS* 12–20), Haribhadra introduces his eightfold analysis of Yoga. He lists eight terms that correlate to Patañjali's limbs of Yoga, and then, as he introduces each one in more detail, he relates each phase to the spiritual systems outlined by Bhadanta Bhāskara and Bhagavaddatta. Though these names appear only in the commentary (presumably written by Haribhadra himself), the consistency of their vocabulary and the underlying philosophy of the terms they chose indicate that the former was a Buddhist and the latter a Vedāntin, to be discussed later. The terms chosen by Haribhadra to describe his eightfold analysis of Yoga are Friendly (Mitrā), Protector (Tārā), Power (Balā), Shining (Dīprā), Firm (Sthirā), Pleasing (Kāntā), Radiant (Prabhā), and Highest (Parā). Each of these names appears in the feminine gender and resonates with the goddess tradition. Haribhadra lists these in a specific order, beginning with a mild form of Yoga and culminating in the most sublime.

For twenty verses (*YDS* 21–40) he describes the foundational practice of Yoga, Friendly, or Mitrā, Yoga. In this exposition, he refers to developing respect for and emulation of the wise, and he suggests that this entails the sloughing off of karmic material. For the next eight verses (*YDS* 41–48) he discusses Protector, or Tārā, Yoga, noting the importance of performing service at this stage. Another seven verses (*YDS* 49–56) are dedicated to Power, or Balā, Yoga, which corresponds to Patañjali's mastery of posture, or *āsana*. Five verses (*YDS* 57–64) discuss Shining, or Dīprā, in terms directly parallel to Patañjali's discussion of the control of breath in his fourth stage.

At this juncture, Haribhadra somewhat changes course. After a brief praise of those persons who listen to truth, devote themselves to a teacher, and purify their understanding, he enters into a critique of what he considers "false" or "inauthentic" views (*YDS* 66–85). As will be discussed in a later chapter, he directly criticizes practices generally associated with Tantra, alluding to the goddess, Durgā. He coins a philosophical term and its opposite: *vedasamvedya/avedasamvedya*, which can be loosely translated as "that which should be perceived" contrasted to "that which should not be perceived." This bears a stark resemblance to the term *avedyavedanīya*, which is used in Bhaṭṭ's commentary on the Laws of Manu, chapter 10, verse 24, to describe prohibited sexual behavior.[2] We have translated this term as *licentiousness*. His language becomes quite vitriolic in this section, suggesting that those who seek pleasure in the name of spiritual liberation are "rendered stupid by the dust of their sin, and never consider truth" (*YDS* 82).

Having criticized Tantric, or Kula, Yoga, an important and a fairly new rival school, Haribhadra then argues for several verses (*YDS* 86–97) against the notion that logic and argument can set one free. He again uses a colorful term, *kutarka*, which translates as a fallacious argument or sophistry to characterize and ridicule the notion that accurate, logical descriptions of the world suffice as true knowledge. He suggests that analogies never bring one close to truth, and that dream knowledge similarly is flawed.

For the next several verses (*YDS* 98–152), Haribhadra addresses a wide range of topics: the importance of following sacred texts, doing good action, and cultivating faith; the singular purity of liberation, despite its various descriptions (discussed in the prior chapter); the contrast between worshipping a god for worldly attainment and devoting oneself to a release from rebirth; the social benefits of sacrificial work; the inviolability of individual integrity; the relationship between intellect and knowledge; the nature of *nirvāṇa*; and the need to respect multiple teachings (also discussed in the prior chapter).

Having held forth on this variety of topics, Haribhadra states, "We are finished now with our digression" (*YDS* 153). He returns to a discussion of the remaining four phases of Yoga, starting with Firm Yoga (Sthirā). His descriptions here closely resemble the corresponding stage in Patañjali, inwardness (*pratyāhāra*), which, like the *Bhagavad Gītā*, emphasizes the maintenance of equanimity and detachment in all one's activities. After nine verses on this topic (*YDS* 153–161), he turns to Pleasing Yoga (Kāntā), which occupies the niche of concentration (*dhāraṇā*) in Patañjali. These eight verses (*YDS* 162–169) indicate that a state of great stability has been attained.

In verses 170 to 177, Haribhadra describes Radiant Yoga (Prabhā) as a stage of great meditation, likening a Yogin to purified gold (*YDS* 174). This level corresponds to Patañjali's discussion of meditation (*dhyāna*). He completes his description of the eight stages with Highest Yoga (Parā), referring to it in verses 178 to 186 as the culmination of the process that began with the eighth Jaina stage (*apūrvakaraṇa guṇasthāna*). He clearly intends to equate Patañjali's *samādhi* to the fourteenth Jaina stage of *ayoga kevala*, mentioned above, at which point all karma disperses. He writes:

> It is said that at the time
> when the clouds of destructive karma
> are themselves destroyed by the wind of Yoga,
> that is the escape.
> Then the glory of singular knowledge is born. (*YDS* 184)

He refers to this state as "highest *nirvāṇa*" and claims that it arises from disjunction (*ayoga*) from all karma (*YDS* 186).

Four additional discourses complete the text of the *Yogadṛṣṭisamuccaya*. The first (*YDS* 187–192) describes the nature of living liberation. The second (*YDS* 193–197) provides a critique of the philosophy of momentariness found in Sarvāstivādin Buddhism. The third (*YDS* 198–203) offers arguments against Vedāntin monism. The final section (*YDS* 204–221) offers a fascinating sociology of Yoga schools, listing five different groups in hierarchical order. As will be explored in the final chapter, he returns to his theme of attempting to subvert the arguments put forward by the Tantrikas. His closing words (*YDS* 222–228) offer this text to be read by those sincerely interested in the study and practice of Yoga, with the intent of removing impediments that stand in the way of one's blessedness.

THE *YOGADṚṢṬISAMUCCAYA* AND JAINISM

The *Yogadṛṣṭisamuccaya* evokes many themes from the Jaina tradition. In the prior chapter, we saw how Haribhadra's methodology gently approaches the views of others, inspired perhaps by the Jaina ethic of nonviolence and the lessons he learned when in philosophical combat with the Buddhists. In subsequent chapters, we will explore the skillful arguments he advances against the Tantrikas, the Sarvāstivādin Buddhists, and the Vedāntins. In each of these instances he does not overtly employ Jaina arguments or rhetoric but reveals what he considers "logical flaws" in each of those respective traditions. In many ways, Haribhadra, in the *Yogadṛṣṭisamuccaya,* seems so relaxed about his Jainism that he seems more like a low Christology Protestant or even a Unitarian than an advocate for Jaina doctrine.

Despite the stealth nature of his Jainism, Haribhadra does employ a few key terms that demonstrate his commitment to Jaina faith and his thorough familiarity with the intricacies of Jaina spiritual philosophy. Though he does not rehearse the Jaina requirements for the core practice of nonviolence (*ahiṃsā*), such as vegetarianism, wearing a mouth covering (*mukhpaṭṭi*), periodic fasting, restriction of movement, and so forth, his generally genial tone and commitment to thinking carefully about the philosophies of rival schools strike the reader of the *Yogadṛṣṭisamuccya* as particularly Jaina in character. However, particularly in his grouping of the eight aspects of Yoga, he clearly attempts to make a connection between Patañjali's path of spirituality and the Jaina path of purification.

Jaina philosophy takes its grounding in its theories of karma. According to the earliest texts of the Jaina tradition, particles of karma bind themselves to the soul (*jīva*) each time one performs an action. The accumulation of these particles causes one to be born again and again within the cycle of birth, death, and rebirth. The only way to reverse these karmic accretions requires adherence to a strict moral code. The *Ācārāṅga Sūtra*, written within a few decades after the death of Mahāvīra, the great Jaina teacher who lived at the same time as the Buddha (ca. 450 to 350 B.C.E.), lists five vows: nonviolence (*ahiṃsā*), truthfulness (*satya*), not stealing (*asteya*), celibacy (*brahmacarya*), and nonpossession (*aparigraha*). These same exact vows form the first limb of Patañjali's eightfold Yoga. According to Jainism, the practice of these five vows allows for the expulsion (*nirjarā*) of karma and advances one toward the state of liberation, referred to in Jainism as *kevala*, or solitariness. Jainism considers the soul eternal, uncreated, and suffused with energy, consciousness, and bliss. Karma obscures its true nature. In the final state of liberation, one abandons all karmic connections and dwells thereafter eternally on one's own mountain peak, perpetually surveying with a dispassionate eye all the things of the world but without attachment or enticement.

The sectarian, textual, and doctrinal history of Jainism is quite long and complicated. Two major groups of Jainas evolved, beginning after a famine (ca. 300 B.C.E.) forced the Jaina community to leave its homeland in northeast India.[3] One group headed to central and south India; it eventually formed the Digambara community. One group headed west, settling in Gujarat and Rajasthan. It came to be known as the Śvetāmbara branch of Jainism, which refers to the white clothing worn by its monks and nuns, as opposed to the Digambara branch, whose more advanced monks wear nothing at all. Though these two groups hold very different views regarding the status of women and do not agree on the authenticity of one another's canons, both accept the writings of the previously mentioned Umāsvāti, an important philosopher who lived in the fifth century. Umāsvāti wrote an important treatise, the *Tattvārtha Sūtra*, that serves as the basis for Jainism as it is studied and practiced today. From its pages emerge the fourteenfold spiritual path, mentioned above, and careful delineations of the various forms of karma and the rather unique Jaina cosmology.[4]

Haribhadra, as noted earlier, did not employ a great deal of Jaina vocabulary in the *Yogadṛṣṭisamuccaya,* nor did he list the rigorous Jaina practices as found in the *Ācārāṅga Sūtra* and other texts. He did, however, attempt to establish a link between his interpretation of Patañjali's eightfold Yoga and the fourteen stages, or *guṇasthānas,* of Jainism. Two terms from the vocabulary of the stages, or *guṇasthānas,* indicate this: the unprecedented (*apūrvakaraṇa*), which refers to actions that are not conditioned by prior afflictions, and disjunction (*ayoga*), a technical term that refers to the ridding of all one's karma. Specifically, Haribhadra states that when one moves from Mitrā to Tārā Yoga, his first two phases, then one moves into the *apūrvakaraṇa*, which is the eighth of the stages, or *guṇasthānas* (verse 39). Earlier he had introduced the concept of unprecedented action (*apūrvakaraṇa*) when making the distinction between dharma renunciation and yoga renunciation. Dharma renunciation, or leaving behind the patterns of life afflicted and determined by karma, takes place prior to the entry into the eighth stage or *guṇasthāna* (verse 10). This would involve cultivating a lifestyle in accordance with the Jaina vows, which takes place primarily in stages, or *guṇasthānas,* four through seven, which will be explained later.

In referring to "Yoga renunciation" (verse 9), Haribhadra does not mean the stoppage of Yoga disciplines. Rather, he is using the term *Yoga* as a synonym for *bandha*, the process of binding karma to the soul. As Y. S. Shastri has noted:

> The subtle particles of matter which flow into the soul and cause its bondage are called Karma. It is Karma that binds the soul to the body. It is caused by the union (*yoga*) of the soul with Pudgala (matter).[5]

While Yoga in Patanjali and related traditions indicates a connection with a higher consciousness, the term *Yoga* in Jainism is used to explain the binding of karma to the soul (*jīva*). The technical definition of Yoga in Jainism is "physical, mental, and vocal activity," while the goal of Jainism is to sever association with such karmic activity through the cessation of Yoga (*yoga-nirodha*).[6] In the first seven stages, or *guṇasthānas*, as we will see, the karmas are controlling one's behavior. Starting with the phase of unprecedented action (*apūrvakaraṇa*), which is Tārā

Yoga, one begins the process of suppressing or releasing and dispelling karmas, the substance, or *dravya,* that Haribhadra refers to in verse 27.

The other term from the stage, or *guṇasthāna,* list that Haribhadra employs is *ayoga,* which first appears in verse eleven (the Yoga of *ayoga* is declared the highest of Yogas) and later appears in verse 186:

> Therein the blessed one quickly attains highest *nirvāṇa*
> through the Yoga of total freedom, the best of Yogas,
> having accomplished the cessation
> of the ailment of worldly existence.

This term directly correlates to the name of the fourteenth *guṇasthāna,* which is *ayoga kevala,* or final liberation from all karma. Hence, if we consider the first of Haribhadra's eight phases to include *guṇasthānas* four through seven, and Haribhadra himself claims that Tārā Yoga corresponds to the stage of unpreceded action or *apūrvakaraṇa,* the eighth *guṇasthāna,* and that Parā Yoga corresponds to *ayoga kevala,* then the intervening stages of Haribhadra's system must correlate to the intervening *guṇasthānas.* (See Table 2.2 for clarification.)

The path of purification in Jainism, as explained by Umāsvāti, begins with the fourth stage, the enlightened worldview, or *saṃyak-dṛṣṭi.* In order to understand the first three stages, we must first gain familiarity with the enlightened worldview, as the first three phases take their meaning only in contrast to this transformative experience. Padmanabh S. Jaini writes eloquently about the enlightened worldview:

> Consciousness attuned only to actions or the results of actions generates perpetual continuation of the samsaric cycle. Upon the attainment of *saṃyak-darśana,* the soul turns away from such concerns; it undergoes a deliberate and mindful reorientation of attention, coming to focus upon nothing but its own nature (*svabhāva*). The body, the possessions, even the ever-changing psychological states (anger, the passions, pride, self-pity, and so forth), are no longer identified with the self. The functioning of consciousness is now characterized as *jñāna-cetanā*; here, the

TABLE 2.2
Haribhadra, Patañjali, and the Guṇasthānas

Haribhadra	Patañjali	Guṇasthāna
Mitrā (Friendly)	Yama (Disciplines)	4–7; insight and ethics
Tārā (Protector)	Niyama (Observances)	8; in path, with passions
Balā (Power)	Āsana (Postures)	9; with gross passions
Dīprā (Shining)	Prāṇāyāma (Control of Breath)	10; with subtle passions
Sthirā (Firm)	Pratyāhāra (Detachment)	11; no passion, calmed delusion, no omniscience
Kāntā (Pleasing)	Dhāraṇā (Concentration)	12; no passion, diminished delusion, no omniscience
Prabhā (Radiant)	Dhyāna (Meditation)	13; no passion, no delusion; with body
Parā (Highest)	Samādhi	14; omniscience, no activity

[Christopher Key Chapple]

individual dwells only upon the innate and pure qualities of the soul, realizing that he is not *doing* anything in the world beyond simply *knowing* it. Finally, his awareness of objects no longer generates a tendency to grasp or manipulate them; he remains in the state called *antarātman*, seeing the self within, thereby greatly increasing his mindfulness and pure awareness. This highly developed *jñāna-*

> *cetanā* will enable him to undertake the pure conduct (*saṃyak-cāritra*) necessary to overcome ingrained negative tendencies, tendencies that have persisted since beginningless time. Thus he will attain eventually to the state of constant self-awareness and purity called *paramātman*, the highest (the liberated) self.[7]

Through this experience, one ascends from the first stage, the realm of wrong views (*mithyā-darśana*). In the first stage, the unenlightened view, one is bound by the karmas of igorance and passion. Because of the heaviness of one's karma, one acts in an unconsciousness manner, continually thickening the density of one's bondage. Ascent to the enlightened worldview "renders the gross passions inoperative and generates sufficient energy in the soul to guarantee rapid progress on the path of conduct."[8] However, one generally does not stay in the fourth stage longer than forty-eight minutes before falling back to the second or third stage.

The second and third stages represent variant forms of backsliding. In stage two (*sāsvādana*), one has had a taste (*svāda*) of the enlightened view, but it has been eclipsed by the reemergence of karmic passions. In the third stage (*saṃyak-mithyātva*), one enters into a state of transition either to or from the enlightened worldview. According to Muni Shri Nyayavijayaji, there is an absence of the most intense passions[9] but a great deal of vacillation, after which one might descend to the first or second stage or reenter the enlightened view. Nathmal Tatia explains this in terms of pure, semi-pure, and impure "heaps" of karma. If pure karma persists, then one remains in the fourth stage and can advance. If semi-pure karma arises, then one relapses into the third stage. If impure karma arises, then one falls down into the second stage and "gradually falls back to the first stage, deluded world-view."[10]

In terms of Haribhadra's threefold analysis of Yoga, a person in the first four stages would be at the first step, or Icchā Yoga. Even if ignorant, she or he might have heard of the spiritual. Once having had the enlightened view, she or he then would perhaps desire to enter into that experience again and, hence, to be within the phase of Wishful Yoga.

The fifth, sixth, and seventh stages comprise an important phase of spiritual resolve that arises from the insights gained during the enlightened worldview. In the fifth stage, restraint according to place (*deśa-virata*), one takes on the vows (*vrata*) taught by the Jaina faith: nonviolence (*ahiṃsā*), truthfulness (*satya*), not stealing (*asteya*), sexual restraint (*brahmacarya*), and nonpossession (*aparigraha*), which are considered the "householder vows." In the sixth stage, total restraint (*sarva-virata, or pramatta-samyata*), one takes on the more rigorous vows of the monk or nun. In the seventh stage, one enters complete restraint (*apramatta-samyata*), overcoming the occasional carelessness in the observance of vows evident in the sixth stage. As noted earlier, these vows, to varying degrees, allow the control or restraint of karmic impulses. They do not, however, involve the total suppression or release or purging of karma. Hence, Haribhadra considers such people to be at the very first stage of Yoga practice, Friendliness, or Mitrā Yoga. For this stage, he lists several activities designed to cultivate the "beginner's mind," including reading books, worship, charity, listening to lectures, studying, and meditating (*YDS* 28). He also gives great words of encouragement directed to persons at that level, seeming to indicate that the entry into the path of purification sets the course for success. In terms of Haribhadra's threefold analysis, they would be at the stage of Precept (Śāstra) Yoga, following the precepts of the great religious teachings.

Haribhadra and Umāsvāti both refer to their next stage (Haribhadra's second, Umāsvāti's eighth) as unprecedented action, or *apūrvakaraṇa*. This rather technical designation refers to the fact that that which had been impure in prior times has been dispelled; the former karma no longer maintains its grip but has been loosened and diminished through the adherence to religious precepts. Haribhadra refers to this second phase as Protector, or Tārā, Yoga. He describes Tārā Yoga as "enabling one to overcome excessive fear and wrong action" (*YDS* 45). Patañjali's equivalent limb, the observances, or *niyamas*, indicates that one takes up deliberate, positive activities: purity, contentment, austerity, study, and dedication to a chosen deity ideal (*śauca, saṃtoṣa, tapas, svādhyāya,* and *īśvara-praṇidhāna*). Von Glasenapp notes that at this, the eighth stage, or *guṇasthāna*, one has fully entered a Śreṇi, or spiritual ladder, and that only white Leśya (color of karma) occurs.[11] However, two paths can be pursued as one leaves the eighth stage. The first, the Suppression Ladder (*upaśama śreṇi*), like the game "Snakes and Ladders," leads one up a couple ladders but then dumps one down into a snake (see frontispiece). It entails the suppression of karma, not its extirpation, and it eventually leads to backsliding. One can ascend along this path to the eleventh stage but then must fall down the snake to stages six, five, four, or two, from which one must start all over again. The second type of unpreceded action, or *apūrvakaraṇa*, the Elimination Ladder (*kṣapaṇa śreṇi*), actually sheds off and extirpates karma and brings one permanently higher, without backsliding. Such a practitioner skips over the perilous eleventh-stage snake and heads straight toward the final goal.

In the ninth stage (*anivṛttikaraṇa guṇasthāna*), one either suppresses or eliminates the secondary passions, listed as sexual feelings (male, female, or mixed), the passions of nonabstinence and partial abstinence, the six quasipassions of "laughter, relish, ennui, grief, fear, and abhorrence," and "flickering anger and pride."[12] In Patañjali, this does not seem to make a tidy match, as Patañjali's third limb focuses on postures, or *āsana*. To the extent that they involve ease and surrender to the infinite, they might be stretched to include rising above the various passions listed; Patañjali writes that this limb, or *āsana,* is "steadiness and ease, from relaxation of effort and endless unity" (*sthira-sukham-āsanam prayatna-śaithilyānanta-samāpattibhyām* [*YS* II:46–47]). Haribhadra describes his third phase of Yoga in terms of Power or Balā Yoga and describes this in terms of qualities of seriousness, which in fact would correspond to the Jaina conquest of the quasipassions:

> Unlike before there is no hastiness
> in all one's goings and activities.
> One is committed to devotion
> and avoids things perishable. (*YDS* 51)

Patañjali also describes *āsana* as resulting in "unassailability by opposites" (*YS* II:48), which, like the verse from Haribhadra, indicates great stability.

In the tenth stage (*sūkṣma-sāmparāya*), one works at suppressing flickering deceit and greed. In Patañjali, this would correspond to *prāṇāyāma*, the fourth limb, which again seems like a bit of a mismatch. However, in Haribhadra's descriptions of his Dīprā Yoga, we see that he emphasizes the purifying powers of correct breathing, stating that through this, one attains accurate perception and purified understanding (*YDS* 65).

The highest stage of suppression (*upaśama*) of karma occurs at the eleventh stage (*upaśānta kaṣāya*). In this, the remaining greed from the tenth stage is eliminated. This stage is required for those who have worked at suppressing karmas, and it will result in falling back into a lower stage, at either the "sixth, fifth, fourth, or to the second stage."[13] Patañjali's fifth stage, withdrawal (*pratyāhāra*), involves a withdrawal from the realm of the senses. Haribhadra names his fifth stage "Firm" or "Sthirā" Yoga:

> Thus those who are firm in their discrimination
> excel at detachment,
> renouncing obstacles to *dharma*
> and exerting genuine effort. (*YDS* 158)

Haribhadra does not directly indicate that this stage entails backsliding, though he does allude to illusion and dream (*YDS* 155, 156) and suggests that anyone who "tries to stop desire through enjoyment" of desire is deluded (*YDS* 161), hinting that one who has achieved the eleventh stage for *guṇasthāna*, which is his fifth stage, is vulnerable.

Those who have genuinely succeeded in eliminating their karmas in stages eight, nine, and ten enter directly into the twelfth stage. This is described by Nathmal Tatia as follows:

> Endowed with great karmic purity, the soul at the ninth stage eliminates the following karmas: the eight passions (four non-abstinence, and four partial-abstinence), the hermaphroditic disposition and the female disposition.[14] The ascetic then eliminates the six quasi-passions (laughter, relish, ennui, grief, fear, abhorrence) by merging them into the male disposition, and then similarly merges the male disposition in flickering anger, flickering anger in

> flickering pride, flickering pride in flickering deceit, and flickering deceit in flickering greed. Then the soul attenuates flickering greed at the tenth stage.[15]

This accomplishment allows one to leap over the perilous eleventh stage (from which one inevitably slides downward) and ascend to the twelfth stage. Hence, in the twelfth stage, one has climbed the Elimination Ladder (*kṣapaṇa-śreṇi*) and attained "complete self-restraint with eliminated passions."[16] In the words of Padmanabh S. Jaini, "the aspirant will reach *kṣīna-moha* [elimination of delusion], permanent disassociation from all the *cāritra-mohanīya* [deluded action] karmas and the passions (*kaṣāya*) which they engender."[17] For Patañjali, this involves a capacity to direct and focus one's thinking in the stage of concentration (*dhāraṇā*). It also comprises the first of the three great "inner Yogas" through which various powers (*siddhis*) are attained. Haribhadra's sixth phase, corresponding to Umāsvāti's twelfth stage, or *guṇasthāna*, is Pleasing, or Kāntā, Yoga, to which he ascribes an ability to move through worldly illusion without becoming attached. He states:

> Just as in seeing the truth behind the illusion of water
> one's mind is put at ease
> and one can go forth quickly through,
> so it is with avoiding obstacles.
> (*YDS* 165)

This simile indicates that the barriers to progress have disappeared, whereas in the prior Yoga, there was an indication of lingering illusions.

The thirteenth stage of Jaina spirituality corresponds to the Hindu notion of the Jīvan Mukta, or the sage who is liberated while living in the world. Tatia translates this stage (*sayoga kevali*) as "omniscience with physical activity."[18] This is said to occur shortly before one's final separation from the body, and it entails a remarkable phase of expansion and contraction.[19] In this phase, one is still connected (*yoga*) to mind, speech, and body, and one still carries the karmas of sensation, name, family group, and life span. Again, though the fit is not exact, Patañjali refers to his seventh limb as meditation (*dhyāna*), said to arise when the mind is able to stay fixed for a long period of time, leading to the final phase of *samādhi*. Haribhadra calls his penultimate stage "Radiant," or "Prabhā," Yoga, which he describes in terms similar to those employed for the person at the stage of *sayoga kevali*:

> This truly perfect stage allows one
> to stand unattached in the midst of attachment.
> The one who follows this great path
> arrives at the stage of not returning. (*YDS* 175)

Haribhadra also includes several verses that describe the nature of living liberation, stating that such a person has been liberated from "giving birth without beginning to the cause of various *karmas*" (*YDS* 189).

The final stage of the Jaina path is referred to as the disembodied state of liberation (*ayogi kevali*), which occurs just prior to death. As expressed by Padmanabh S. Jaini: "At the instance of death (*nirvāṇa*) itself, the soul is freed forever from the last vestige of samsaric influence; thus it reaches in the very next moment the state of infinite bliss and omniscience called siddha."[20] The remaining karmas are annihilated and, as described by von Glasenapp,

> Relieved of all matter, the soul ascends in a straight line during a samaya (instant) to the summit of the world, as a gourd freed from all filth no longer sinks to the bottom but rises to the surface of the water.
>
> High above the Sarvārthasiddhi-heaven, close to the border between world and no-world, lies the magnificent region of *Iṣatprāgbhārā*, in a shape like an unfolded sunshade. Thereto the blessed betake themselves in order to settle down permanently in the uppermost part of it, in Śītā. Without visible shape, bodiless, but a dimension in space (immaterial) of 2/3 of that which they had had during their last existence, they dwell there thenceforward into all eternity, and enjoy the infinite, incomparable, indestructible supernatural happiness of salvation.[21]

The final state, the goal of the tradition, has been attained. In terms of Patañjali's *Yoga Sūtra*, it would correspond to the final state of *nirbīja samādhi*, the culmination of several levels of *samādhi*, ranging from with form/thought, without form/thought, with reflection, without reflection, with seed, and finally without seed, at which point all afflictions and fluctuations cease. Haribhadra clearly regards his final Yoga phase, Highest, or Parā, Yoga, to correlate to the fourteenth stage, or *guṇasthāna*, as indicated in the use of the term *ayoga*, mentioned above, and in his descriptions:

> This is the culmination born
> of the second *apūrvakaraṇa*
> (that is, the Elimination Ladder).
> This has the radiance of *kevala* (perfect knowledge).
> Freedom from all adversity arises. (*YDS* 182)
>
> With faults eliminated, omniscient,
> endowed with the fruits
> of all that can be accomplished,
> with things to be done now only for the sake of others,
> such a one attains the end of Yoga. (*YDS* 185)
>
> Therein the blessed one quickly attains highest *nirvāṇa*,
> through the Yoga of total freedom, the best of Yogas,
> having accomplished the cessation
> of the ailment of worldly existence. (*YDS* 186)

All karmas have been expelled, and the soul has achieved liberation. [See Table 2.3]

Haribhadra's eight limbs nicely correspond to the eight highest stages, or *guṇasthānas*, of Umāsvāti. He has been somewhat less successful in fitting Patañjali's stages into the Jaina scheme, aside from acknowledging the identity of the *vrata*s and the *yama*s and equating Patañjali's description of *nirbīja samādhi* to the Jaina stage of *ayogi kevala*. His own eightfold goddess system follows Patanjali's eight limbs and also correlates to the *guṇasthāna* scheme, eight through fourteen. However, to align the *guṇasthāna* scheme with the *Yoga Sūtra*, it would be far better to look at the stages of *samādhi* mentioned in the first section of the *Yoga Sūtra* than to try to align the *guṇasthānas* with the stages of Yoga listed in the second section of the *Yoga Sūtra*.

TABLE 2.3
Spiritual Ascent through the Guṇasthāna(s)

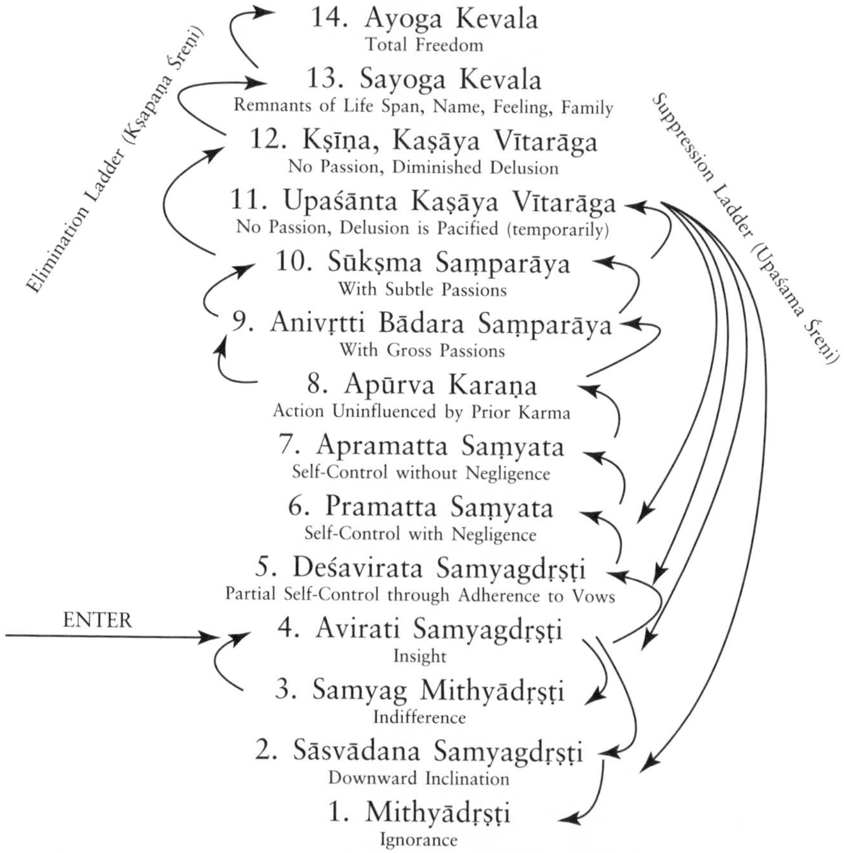

[Christopher Key Chapple]

In the *samādhi pāda*, as summarized earlier, Patañjali first outlines the workings of the mind and then lists a variety of practices bringing about the state of yoga, defined as the "suppression of fluctuations in the mind" (*citta-vṛtti-nirodha*). This list includes practice and dispassion, the Brahma Vihāra, devotion to the Lord of Yoga (Īśvara), and a host of other practices. In terms of the *guṇasthāna* system, these might be equated to the first seven stages: rising above the ignorant view, making a decision to purify one's life, and establishing oneself in foundational ethical practices. At the conclusion of this list of some twenty or so practices, Patañjali then enters into a systematic discourse on the hierarchy of stages of *samādhi*. He begins with a description of the core experience of *samāpatti*, moving into a state of clarity between grasper, grasping, and grasped, so that one's consciousness, like a clear jewel, becomes transparent (*YS* I:41). In terms of the *guṇasthānas*, this state would involve fully moving into a transformative spiritual path. In the words of Gurāṇi Añjali, "spiritual life begins with *samādhi.*" The next phase is *savitarka samādhi*, described as concentration with a gross object. In terms of the *guṇasthānas*, this might refer to the ninth stage, defined as "with gross passions." Patañjali next describes *nirvitarka*, or concentration without a gross object, correlating to the tenth *guṇasthāna*, with subtle passions. On the next level, Patañjali discusses *savicāra samādhi*, a form of concentration with a subtle object, which could correspond to the eleventh *guṇasthāna*, which, as we saw earlier, holds an important transitional place in Jainism. In Patañjali, this is followed with *nirvicāra*, an objectless form of subtle concentation that helps erase prior karmic impressions (*saṃskāras*) and, in the words of the commentator, Vyāsa, turn them into sterile "burnt seeds." This would correspond perhaps to the twelfth *guṇasthāna*, during which the passions disappear, and delusions have been minimized. At the thirteenth and fourteenth levels, one enters into a state of liberation, first with the body and then without. The thirteenth stage could correspond to *sabīja samādhi,* with the seeds, or *bījas,* perhaps referring to the final four karmas of Jainism. *Ayogakevala,* or total freedom, could correspond to the fourteenth and final stage of seedless (*nirbīja*) *samādhi*, which results in first the restriction of other karmic impressions and finally the suppression of everything (*sarva-nirodha*). The expulsion of subtle karma through the sevenfold application of *samādhi* seems closer to the Jaina *guṇasthāna* system than the limbs mentioned by Patañjali in his eightfold system (see Table 2.4).

In this chapter we have investigated Haribhadra's attempts to align his interpretations of Yoga within the context of Patañjali's Yoga, and Jaina *guṇasthāna* theory, using two words in the *Yogadṛṣṭisamuccaya* that seem to give obvious clues. The term

TABLE 2.4
The Progressive Erasure of Karma

	Jainism's Guṇasthānas	Patañjali's Samādhis
1–7.	ignorance, insight, and ethics	citta-vṛtti
8.	Apūrva Karaṇa Action uninfluenced by prior karma	samāpatti
9.	Anivṛtti Bādara Saṃparāya with gross passions	savitarka
10.	Sūkṣma Saṃparāya with subtle passions	nirvitarka
11.	Upaśānta Kaṣāya Vītarāga No passion, delusion temporarily pacified	savicāra
12.	Ksīṇa Kaṣāya Vītarāga No passion, diminished delusion	nirvicāra
13.	Sayoga Kevala Remnants of Karma	sabīja
14.	Ayoga Kevala Total Freedom	nirbīja

[Christopher Key Chapple]

apūrvakaraṇa, used in reference to Haribhadra's second stage (Tārā), is used in the commentaries on Umāsvāti's *Tattvārtha Sūtra* to refer to the eighth *guṇasthāna*. The term *ayoga* is used to describe the eighth and final of Haribhadra's stages. In Umāsvāti, the same term is used to describe the fourteenth and final *guṇasthāna*. Using these two clues, it has been argued that the eight stages of Haribhadra's Yoga correlate to the upper eight levels of the *guṇasthāna* system.[22] In the next chapter, we will examine his attempt to explain the Yoga systems of Bhadanta Bhāskara and Bandhu Bhagavaddatta, which seem to be affiliated with Buddhism and Vedānta, respectively.

CHAPTER THREE

The Vedāntin Yoga of Bhagavaddatta and the Buddhist Yoga of Bhāskara

In the *Yogadṛṣṭisamuccaya*, Haribhadra describes three systems of Yoga for which we have no other account. The first is attributed to Haribhadra himself and incorporates terminology reflective of the Tantric movement that flourished during his time, as will be discussed in chapter six. The other two are attributed in the autocommentary (verse 16) to Bandhu Bhagavaddatta and Bhadanta Bhāskara. Though I have searched various sources, from Hemacandra's *Abhidhānacintāmaṇi* to Tson Kha Pa's *Lam Rim Chen Mo*, and have consulted numerous international scholars, there is apparently no other record for these persons, nor do their articulations of Yoga align with any other systems. However, in the section that follows, I will hypothesize about their doctrinal affiliations, suggesting that Bandhu Bhagavaddatta hails from a Brahmanical or Śaivite or Vedāntin school of thought, and that Bhadanta Bhāskara was a teacher of Buddhism. In the following chapter, I will then examine the arguments in the *Yogadṛṣṭisamuccaya* that challenge Brahmanical and Buddhist positions and explore how the inclusion of these two thinkers relates to Haribhadra's mission of unifying all truth under the rubric of the common goal of liberation.

In the *Yogadṛṣṭisamuccaya*, the Vedāntin and Buddhist systems of Yoga are listed as parallel components to Patañjali's and Haribhadra's eightfold paths. The systems attributed to Bandhu

Bhagavaddatta and Bhadanta Bhāskara in the commentary on verse sixteen are described over a sequence of verses that mention the eight limbs (*angas*) of Patañjali. Haribhadra names correlative yoga practices for each of the four systems: his own, as discussed in the prior chapter, Patañjali, Bhagavaddatta, and Bhāskara.[1]

In the prior chapter I explored the relationship between Haribhadra's eight yogas, Patañjali's eight limbs, and the Jaina stages of spirituality, or *guṇasthānas*. In this chapter, I attempt to isolate the Vedāntic and Buddhist systems attributed to Bhagavaddatta and Bhāskara. By looking at each first in the context of its appearance in Haribhadra and then advancing a cogent vocabulary reflective of Brahmanical and Buddhist ideology, respectively, I hope to recover the intention and possible application of these "Lost Yogas." In chapter four I explore how these renderings or interpretations of Brahmanical and Buddhist ideology reflect Haribhadra's own understanding of Brahmanism and Buddhism, and how they might possibly serve his purposes of criticizing Brahmanical "monism" and Buddhist "nihilism" elsewhere in the text.

THE EIGHTFOLD VEDĀNTIN YOGA OF BANDHU BHAGAVADDATTA

In his commentary on verse 16, Haribhadra attributes an eightfold scheme of Yoga to a scholar he names "Bandhu Bhagavaddatta." A search of various catalogues and other bibliograhic listings has yielded no such author as early as the eighth century, so it can only be assumed that Bhagavaddatta either was the author of texts that have since been lost or a prominent teacher during the time of Haribhadra, or both. According to Sanghavi, he might have been a Śaiva or Paśupata teacher.[2] His name, which means "God Given," indicates a theistic orientation, and many of the eight categories that he lists reflect Brahmanical textual traditions. By listing and describing each level in terms of both its core vocabulary and elaborations made by Haribhadra in the autocommentary and subsequent verses, I attempt a reconstruction of this eightfold Yoga path.

TABLE 3.1
Forms of Yoga as Given in Haribhadra's *Yogadṛṣṭisamuccaya*

Haribhadra	Patañjali	Bandhu Bhagavaddatta	Bhadanta Bhāskara
Mitrā (Friendly)	Yama (Disciplines)	Adveṣa (No Aversion)	Akheda (No Distress)
Tārā (Protector)	Niyama (Observances)	Jijñāsa (Desire for Knowledge)	Anudvega (No Anxiety)
Balā (Power)	Āsana (Postures)	Śuśrūṣā (Desirous to Hear Truth)	Akṣepa (No Distraction)
Dīprā (Shining)	Prāṇāyāma (Control of Breath)	Śravaṇa (Hearing Truth)	Anuttānavatī (No Interruption)
Sthirā (Firm)	Pratyāhāra (Detachment)	Sukṣmabodha (Subtle Awakening)	Abhrānti (Unmuddied)
Kāntā (Pleasing)	Dhāraṇā (Concentration)	Mīmāṃsā (Reflection)	Ananyamud (Not Finding Pleasure in Anything Other)
Prabhā (Radiant)	Dhyāna (Meditation)	Pratipatti (Perception of Truth)	Arug (Without Pain)
Parā (Highest)	Samādhi	Sātmī-kṛta-pravṛtti (Enactment of Absorption)	Saṅga Vivarjitā (Free from Attachment)

[Christopher Key Chapple]

The first term used by Bhagavaddatta is *adveṣa*, which I have translated as "freedom from aversion." Like *ahiṃsā* (nonviolence), *asteya* (not stealing), and *aparigraha* (nonpossession) within Patañjali's first stage, this is stated in negative terms. Rather than putting forward a positive term such as equanimity (*sama*) or peacefulness (*śānti*), Bhagavaddatta states what is to be avoided. This interesting device, widely employed by the Buddhists (as we will see later), operates from the premise that something is awry, and that steps must be taken to reverse it. In this instance, aversion or dislike first must be recognized and then overcome. In the commentary, Haribhadra lists as a synonym the term *amatsara*, which means unenvious or disinterested. Both terms indicate a state of detachment or dispassion. This concept of rising above aversion finds prominence throughout the *Bhagavad Gītā* in such verses as II:64, which speaks of being free from aversion and desire, and V:3, which proclaims that the one who "neither hates nor desires, is to be known as the everlasting renouncer (*sannyāsi*)."[3]

The subsequent terms used by Bhagavaddatta are couched in a more positive modality and evoke ideas also found in a wide range of texts and traditions in the years prior to Haribhadra. The first of these terms, *jijñāsā*, "desirous of knowledge," is rooted in a desiderative form. It is followed with the terms indicating the field of one's reality (*tattvagocara*), indicating that, as in Śankara's *Atmabodha* and Iśvarakṛṣṇa's *Sāṃkhya Kārikā*, among countless other texts, an intentionality fixed on spiritual knowledge is essential. The commentary states that this arises after *adveṣa*.

The third phase of Patañjali's Yoga is the accomplishment of *āsana*, free and steady placement of the body. In later tradition, this becomes closely associated with the Haṭha Yoga schools and refers to the wide range of postures that the aspiring yogi learns in an attempt to prepare the body for extended periods of meditation. In Bhagavaddatta, this third stage is called *śuśrūṣā*, which I have translated as "desirous to hear truth." It follows the same desiderative structure as the prior phase, and again it echoes

TABLE 3.2
The Yoga of Bandhu Bhagavaddatta

Adveṣa (No Adversion)
Jijñāsa (Desire for Knowledge)
Śuśrūṣā (Desirous to Hear Truth)
Śravaṇa (Hearing Truth)
Sukṣmabodha (Subtle Awakening)
Mīmāṃsā (Reflection)
Pratipatti (Perception of Truth)
Sātmī-kṛta–pravṛtti (Enactment of Absorption)

many texts that refer to the need for one to be teachable in order to progress on the spiritual journey.

In the commentary, Haribhadra states that "desirous to hear truth" would be the same as the "desire for knowledge." However, in the root text, he later expands on this notion, drawing the analogy that desiring to hear truth is like the heavenly songs that young lovers hear when joined together (*YDS* 52). He further intimates that this truth is to be found in scripture (*śrutam*) (*YDS* 53). In neither the commentary nor the later root text references to this stage does Haribhadra refer to *āsana* as a form of physical movement. This might reflect the actual practice of Yoga at the time (as noted earlier, the Haṭha Yoga manuals probably arise at a later date), or traditional Jaina indifference to purely "physical" yoga.

Bhagavaddatta refers to the fourth stage as "hearing truth" (*śravaṇa*). In the commentary, Haribhadra says this is the result (*phalam*) of the desire to hear truth. However, unlike the prior stage, Haribhadra explicitly links this accomplishment to the parallel level in Patañjali. He proclaims that one who hears highest truth goes "from strength of the breaths, indeed, to the highest dharma" (*YDS* 60). He also draws an analogy that one who seeks truth will flourish like a sprouting seed in fresh water, while the worldly one will perish like a sprout in salt water (*YDS* 61, 62).

The fifth stage of Bhagavaddatta is called *sūkṣmabodha*, or "subtle awakening," which corresponds to what Patañjali terms *pratyāhāra*, in which one detaches from the objects of the senses. Though Patañjali chooses to refer to this state in somewhat negative terms, Haribhadra, in his explication, expresses this level in more positive terms. He states that this phase corresponds to "the cutting of the knot" (*granthi-bheda*), which indicates that here one begins to effectively disengage from the snares of particular karmas. He also links this phase to *vedyasaṃvedyapada*, the special term coined by Haribhadra to indicate the correct path. To illustrate the spiritual import of this critical fifth phase, he uses several metaphors:

> Through the undoing of the knot of lethargy,
> the entire struggle of worldly existence
> is perceived by the wise as like children
> playing with a house made of sand.

One sees all external existence
as if it resembles a dream,
the city of the Gandharvas, a magician's illusion.
Here the only thing resembling truth
is the interior, singular, undisturbed, unnameable light;
anything else is merely a disturbance. (*YDS* 155–157)

Having communicated the positive spiritual aspects of this accomplishment, he then explains this subtle awakening in more traditional language, emphasizing the need to renounce attachment to physicality:

Thus those who are firm in their discrimination
excel at detachment,
renouncing obstacles to *dharma*
and exerting genuine effort.
For the wise, wealth does not bring happiness,
because its friend is poverty.
So should it be for the many
extensive enjoyments of the body,
which in the world have sin as their companion.
(*YDS* 158–159)

At the level of the inner limbs of Yoga, Haribhadra's descriptions become quite animated. He enthusiastically establishes commonalities between all the systems that he juxtaposes. This corresponds to his assessment that these phases of Yoga are truly effective, while the possibility of backsliding exists within the prior four stages.

The sixth phase of Patañjali's Yoga is concentration (*dhāraṇā*), the first component required for the advanced technique of *saṃyama*. In Patañjali, the simultaneous application of concentration, meditation, and *samādhi* leads to great spiritual accomplishments (*siddhi*) and eventually to the state of discriminative discernment (*viveka khyāti*) and liberation (*kaivalyam*). For Bhagavaddatta, this phase is interestingly termed *Mīmāṃsā*, which I have translated as "reflection." In traditional Hinduism, *Mīmāṃsā* is the name of the philosophical school that deals with the particulars of enacting Vedic sacrifice. The inclusion of this title does not refer specifically to this extensive tradition but probably indicates value being placed on a concern for proper sustenance of a particular worldview. By viewing life in ritual categories, the propensity to cling to karmic structures lessens. In the performance of ritual, the creation of positive *saṃskāras* in accordance with religious precepts can help minimize worldly *saṃskāras*.

Etymologically, the term *mīmāṃsā* derives from a desiderative form of the root *man*, "to think." It indicates a desire to think on a more profound level. In his commentary, Haribhadra states that it refers to reflection or cogitation on the real by one's self (*sad-vicāra-ātmikā*). By introducing a term used by Patañjali to describe a preliminary state of concentration (see *YS* I:44 on *savicāra, nirvicāra*, etc.), and by using an epithet for Brahman (*sat*) and a reference to the notion of Self, Haribhadra establishes this phase within the Brahmanical theological tradition.

In the verses that explicate Haribhadra's understanding of this sixth phase, he states that one's conduct becomes purified, that one is beloved among beings, with a mind always fixed on scriptural teachings. Such a one, he states, no longer becomes enticed by worldly affairs and avoids obstacles as though they were only a mirage. As with descriptions of the liberated soul in the *Chāndogya Upaniṣad* and the extensive Living Liberation (*jīvanmukti*) tradition of later Vedānta, he states that one remains detached even while in the midst of enjoyment, progressing toward the highest step.

Bhagavaddatta refers to the seventh and penultimate stage as *Tattva Pratipatti*, which I translate as "perception of truth." Though Haribhadra provides no commentary for the verse in which this stage is mentioned, it is clear from its context and the verses that follow that he equates this stage to Patañjali's Meditation (*dhyāna*). The benefits that accrue are quite similar to those listed for the prior stage, though more intense:

> In this, happiness is born of meditation,
> as well as the discipline of conquering amorous passion,
> the emergence of strong discrimination,
> and the power of constant serenity. (*YDS* 171)

He also describes this state as being beyond concern for merit, and he notes that the great souls meditate because of their purified intellect.

For the eighth and final stage of Yoga, Bhagavaddatta introduces a new term, *sa-ātmī-kṛta-pravṛtti*, which I translate as "Enactment of Absorption." In this phase, all things are done without separation from one's true self. Haribhadra's commentary cites several of Patañjali's aphorisms that describe concentration, meditation, and samādhi, and though he does not fully define Bhagavaddatta's phrase, "Enactment of Absorption," he does include in his descriptions of liberation the notion that the enactment of this state is like the smell of sandalwood, that is, the best.

The verses that follow equate the eighth stage to liberation and freedom from all adversity. Such a person's consciousness is said to be "like a cloud concealing the moonlight" (*YDS* 183). The person in the eighth stage does things only for the sake of others (*YDS* 185). Though using epithets from Buddhist, Jaina, and Hindu modes of expression, Haribhadra does not seem to give priority to one tradition over another. However, the term Enactment of Absorption (*sātmīkṛtapravṛtti*) attributed to Bhagavaddatta for this highest form of Yoga is particularly noteworthy for its positivistic slant, in contrast to the theologically neutral term used by Patañjali (*samādhi*), the theologically specific term used by the Jainas (*kevala*), and the decidedly nontheistic, nonsubtantialist term used by the Buddhists (*saṅga vivarjitā*).

In concluding our discussion of Bhagavaddatta, the following points can be made. He uses terms familiar to the Upaniṣadic and Brahmanical tradition and names that could be readily found in the *Gītā*, the Upaniṣads, the names of schools, and so on. He uses the desiderative form repeatedly, which perhaps was a favorite of the learned Brahmins. He most likely emphasizes scripture, as indicated in the verses used by Haribhadra to explicate each of the levels. Although we have no information about Bhagavaddatta outside of Haribhadra's rendering, it seems clear that he represents a Brahmanical perspective, with leanings toward the school that later came to be identified as "Advaita Vedānta."

THE EIGHTFOLD BUDDHIST YOGA OF BHADANTA BHĀSKARA

Along with his own rendering of eightfold Yoga, Patañjali's eightfold system, and the eightfold Yoga attributed to Bandhu

Bhagavaddatta, Haribhadra also explicates an eightfold Yoga that the commentary attributes to Bhadanta Bhāskara. As with Bhagavaddatta, we have no external confirmation for the life or work of Bhāskara. However, by looking at his name and then at some generic features of how he describes Yoga, we may glean a sense of his identity and religious persuasion. First, the prefix to his name, Bhadanta, is a term of respect usually reserved for Buddhist monks. In the Pāli tradition, this appelation becomes abridged to Bhante, a form of address found throughout Buddhist literature. His presumed given name, Bhāskara, is shared with scholars of the Hindu tradition several centuries after Haribhadra. However, due to the honorific term *Bhadanta*, and from the study of the content of his thought as follows, it can be speculated that Bhāskara was most likely a Buddhist teacher of Yoga.[4] As with Bhagavaddatta, a reconstruction of Bhāskara's Yoga will be attempted through an analysis of its core vocabulary, Haribhadra's commentary, and related passages from the main text.

The first term used by Bhāskara, *akheda*, has been translated as "freedom from distress," and it is said to be "related to the gods." In the commentary Haribhadra explains that this linkage to the gods in fact refers to holding to the primal words (*ādiśabda*) made by the teacher. It states: "From time to time, one falls from happiness into a state of distress. The reality of this primal fault, according to the head teacher, [leads one to] greater delight and enjoyment (as found in Yoga)."[5] In many ways, this commentary appears to restate the first teaching of the Buddha, that all reality is fraught with suffering, and that this suffering prompts one to seek release. This concern for the teacher also is reflected in verse 26, which advises that "devotion is to be directed especially to teachers and the like; in such yogis arises a state of purity." This analysis of the role of the teacher, that is, to provide a model for and counsel to those who suffer, is an important characteristic of the religious traditions of India.

Bhāskara describes the second phase of his eightfold Yoga as a state of being free from anxiety (*anudvega*) while involved in undertakings. The commentary explains this as a state of not being distressed about things to happen in the world to come (*pāralaukike akhedasahitaḥ*). Haribhadra later describes this second phase of Yoga as a state where fear becomes abolished, yet

TABLE 3.3
The Yoga of Bhadanta Bhāskara

Akheda (No Distress)
Anudvega (No Anxiety)
Akṣepa (No Distraction)
Anuttānavatī (No Interruption)
Abhrānti (Unmuddied)
Ananyamud (Not Finding Pleasure in Anything Other)
Arug (Without Pain)
Saṅga Vivarjitā (Free from Attachment)

[Christopher Key Chapple]

one may still undertake activities: "there is no abandonment of what should be done. Even when neglectful, these lofty ones do no improper action" (*YDS* 45).

The third phase of Yoga, as characterized by Bhāskara, involves being free from distraction (*akṣepa*). Although his commentary gives no elaboration other than to say that this state arises from the prior one, two later verses explain the significance of overcoming distraction:

> In undertaking this Yoga of purification,
> there is never any vacillation.
> And, indeed, the path of purity
> would be the beloved (object) sphere.
> For one who has gone forth
> on this path of self-discipline,
> obstacles are not known.
> This absence of obstacles
> due to a shunning of objectionable things
> is liberation. (*YDS* 55–56)

By leaving behind distraction, one gains the discipline needed to overcome impediments to liberation.

Bhadanta Bhāskara characterizes the fourth phase of Yoga, correlating to Patañjali's control of breath (*prāṇāyāma*), as a state without interruption (*na yoga utthānavatī*). The commentary explains that one arrives at this state through the attainment of a calm disposition or comportment (*tathā vidha praśānta vāhitā lābhena*).

The fifth phase, which as noted earlier indicates a transition into the more powerful "inner forms" of Yoga (*antaraṅga*), is characterized by Bhaskara as "unmuddied" (*abhrānti*), which also could be referred to as "nondeluded" or "unerring." The commentary defines actions undertaken at this phase as respectful (*vandanādi*), stating in this context that they are sanctioned from above (*kramamadhikṛtya*) and are without sin (*anaghamana*) because of their elevated nature (*aticāratvāt*).[6]

Bhāskara describes the sixth phase (Patañjali's concentration) as not finding pleasure in the other (*ananyamud*). The commentary states that this meaning is obvious, and later in the main text, he elaborates on the nature of the "other," writing:

> Again, one for whom enjoyments are real
> never crosses over the ocean of existence.
> After firmly immersing oneself in the waters of illusion,
> how is one able to go on the path? (*YDS* 167)

The deluded person sees the world as exterior and oppositional to herself or himself. By extricating oneself from the notion that the other is in fact separate from oneself, then obstacles can be dispelled (*YDS* 165).

The state of meditation, or *dhyāna*, Patañjali's seventh phase, is characterized in Bhāskara as "without pain" (*arug*). Though Haribhadra provides no comment on this verse, the following verses convey the spirit of both the sixth and seventh stages, as articulated by Bhāskara:

> "All suffering [is dependent on] externals;
> all happiness [is dependent on] oneself."
> This saying, in brief, [gives]
> the characteristics of pleasure and pain.
> Even what appears to be merit in fact
> is situated in external happiness.

> Hence, it is actually pain,
> in accordance with this characteristic. (*YDS* 172–173)

Even a person's meritorious acts benefit other people and hence reinforce the notion of another as exterior to oneself. Such action, rather than advancing oneself or another toward liberation, actually can be an occasion for further attachment.

Implying that it is better to remain inactive rather than actively seeking to help others, Haribhadra writes that the "great souls meditate" and, as an introduction to the final stage, he notes that:

> This truly perfect stage allows one
> to stand unattached in the midst of attachment.
> The one who follows this great path
> arrives at the stage of not returning. (*YDS* 175)

By not seeking to reach out to others, and by remaining satisfied within oneself, one approaches the final stage of Yoga.

Bhāskara describes the eighth stage of Yoga as free from attachment (*saṅga vivarjitā*). In the commentary he specifies that this entails breaking free from the activities of the world (*bhūtapravṛtti*). Haribhadra describes this state of detachment with several analogies:

> The behavior of such a one
> is like the manner of one who,
> having climbed up [a mountain]
> no longer is in the state of climbing.
> Just as one who is trained in looking at jewels and
> so forth
> is different from the one who is merely enjoined
> to look at them,
> so the action and conduct of such a one are different
> due to the distinction of the fruit it bears. (*YDS* 179–180)

The "distinct fruit" in this case would refer to the fact that the actions of the liberated one are completely disinterested. No longer concerned for his or her own well-being, the goal has been achieved, allowing such a person to act purely for the sake of others, with no selfish intent:

> With faults eliminated, omniscient,
> endowed with the fruits of all that can be accomplished,
> with things to be done now only for the sake of others,
> such a one attains the end of Yoga.
> Therein the blessed one quickly attains highest *nirvāṇa*
> through the Yoga of Total Freedom,
> the best of Yogas, having accomplished the cessation
> of the ailment of worldly existence. (*YDS* 185–186)

These verses in particular use Buddhist terminology and imagery to describe the final state of Yoga, and hence they can be reasonably linked to the thought of Bhadanta Bhāskara.

In summary, Bhadanta Bhāskara seems to present Buddhist approaches to Yoga in several ways. First, all of his terminology is couched in negative language. With the exception of the more grammatically complex eighth stage, the descriptions of all of his Yoga practices begin with the negating prefix "a." Second, he makes the centrality of suffering, as found in Buddhism, the key to his argument, both in his explication of the spiritual importance of discomfort in his explanation of the first stage, and in his subsequent reminders of the pain of existence that arises from the delusion that one can help another person. In describing the state of being free from attachment as the highest Yogic goal, Haribhadra uses explicitly Buddhist terminology, including the term *nirvāṇa*.

The Vedāntin Yoga of Bandhu Bhagavaddatta begins with a turning away from adverse situations. From this one cultivates a desire for knowledge, followed by a desire to hear truth and the hearing of truth. This results in a subtle awakening, his fifth stage. From reflection arises the perception of truth, culminating in the joining with one's true self in the midst of one's activities (*sātmī-kṛta-pravṛtta*). The Buddhist Yoga of Bhadanta Bhāskara similarly begins with turning away from distress. In sequence, one moves beyond anxiety, distractions, and interruptions to arrive at the fifth stage, referred to as "unmuddied." After mastering a sense of completion within oneself (*ananyamud*), one transcends pain, and in the culminating final eighth phase, one lives free from attachment (*saṅga vivarjitā*).

In his explication of these three thinkers, Haribhadra skillfully demonstrates how two very different Hindu thinkers (Patañjali and Bhagavaddatta) and a Buddhist thinker (Bhāskara) can arrive at the same goal of liberation, using very different modalities of practice. However, he does not necessarily agree with the philosophical frameworks that undergird Bhagavaddatta and Bhāskara. In the next chapter, we explore his critique of the momentariness theories of Buddhism and the monistic theories of the Upaniṣads.

CHAPTER FOUR

Centrality of the Real

Jainism's core religious philosophy, as articulated by Umāsvāti in the *Tattvārtha Sūtra*, asserts that the world is real, that the soul is real, and that the religious path involves a gradual ascent through sequential stages (*guṇasthāna*), away from the influences of karma and toward final liberation. The insistence on the reality of the world distinguishes Jainism from Vedāntic forms of Hinduism. The second assertion regarding the reality of the soul distinguishes Jainism from Buddhism. The third aspect of Jainism, the notion of successive stages of spirituality (*guṇasthānas*), as articulated in Umāsvāti's *Tattvārtha Sūtra*, brings Jainism into accordance with some of the meditative traditions of Buddhism and Yoga. However, because these three Śrāmaṇical traditions of Yoga, Buddhism, and Jainism are grounded in radically different theological views, they remain distinct: Yoga allows for the possibility of a meditative ideal that carries theistic overtones and makes positive statements regarding the human self; Buddhism disallows any positive allusion to theism or self; and Jainism posits countless souls involved with a quest to disengage themselves from karma.

Haribhadra was familiar with all the schools of thought mentioned above: Vedānta, Yoga, Buddhism, and Jainism. In his surveys of religious philosophy, he seems to affirm aspects of each, emphasizing the importance of liberation (*nirvāṇa* or *mokṣa*) to all of them. In both of his major Sanskrit texts on Yoga, the *Yogadṛṣṭisamuccaya* and the *Yogabindu*, he emphasizes the importance of acknowledging the reality of existence and its concomitant sorrows as a prerequisite for entering the path of liberation. In this chapter, I discuss passages from both texts that assert the centrality of the real in Jainism and demonstrate how Haribhadra uses this touchstone to distinguish the Jaina position from views held by Buddhists and Vedāntins.

In the *Yogadṛṣṭisamuccaya*, Haribhadra presents a comparative account of different schools of Yoga. In the process he creates an architectonic scheme by which these multiple disciplines are juxtaposed and put forth as alternate paths to the same goal of karmic dispersal. As mentioned in the first chapter, he states that regardless of the tradition, the state of liberation is constant, as indicated in the following verses:

> The highest essence of going beyond *saṃsāra*
> is called *nirvāṇa*.
> The wisdom gained from discipline
> is singular in essence,
> though heard of in different ways.
> "Eternal Śiva, Highest Brahman, Accomplished Soul, Suchness":
> with these words one refers to it,
> though the meaning is one
> in all the various forms. (*YDS* 129–30)

By holding forth *nirvāṇa* as the goal of various religious systems, Haribhadra posits a commonality of purpose among religious traditions. As was discussed in the first chapter, other scholars of Haribhadra have suggested that this approach to faiths other than Jainism indicates a high degree of liberality, though, as I will discuss later in this chapter, elsewhere in the *Yogadṛṣṭisamuccaya* Haribhadra refutes the philosophical premises of non-Jaina schools, even though they share the common *telos* of liberation.

The drive toward homologizing and harmonizing diverse religious traditions and practices has surfaced frequently in the history of Indian thought, most recently in the guise of neo-Vedānta, a universalist form of Hinduism. This tendency also is evident in the *Yogavāsiṣṭha*, a vast Hindu text in the process of being compiled during the lifetime of Haribhadra, in the tradition of what I call "monistic accommodationism." Rather than defining a firm position that is "owned" by the author, the *Yogavāsiṣṭha* exhibits an exuberant affirmation of diversity. Siding with what can, in modern times, be referred to as "perennialists," the *Yogavāsiṣṭha* proposes that all mystics share a transcendental state of consciousness without an object:

> a state of bliss that is not its description, which is both the "is" and the "is not," both something and non-something, light and darkness. It is full of non-consciousness and consciousness. It can only be indicated by negation. . . . That state is the void, Brahman, consciousness, the Puruṣa of the Sāṃkhya, Īśvara of the Yogi, Śiva, time, Ātman or self, nonself and the middle, and so forth. It is that state which is established as the truth by all these scriptural viewpoints, that which is all. In that, the sage remains firmly established.[1]

The *Yogavāsiṣṭha* describes the absolute as "the Puruṣa of the Sāṃkhya philosophers, the Brahman of the Vedāntins, the Vijñānamātra of the Yogācāra Buddhists, and the Śūnya of the Śūnyavādins,"[2] making a home within its fold for the dualistic and monistic Hindus and the idealistic and nihilistic Buddhists. The text affirms the Upaniṣadic notion that, "I am the Self of all," yet it also makes Buddhistic statements such as, "It is neither sentient nor insentient, neither being nor non-being, neither ego nor non-ego, neither one nor many."[3] The *Yogavāsiṣṭha* is committed to the notion that a single truth undergirds reality, as posited in the Upaniṣads, but it is also sensitive to the unwillingness of the Buddhist tradition to categorize or name this reality. Consequently, it celebrates Buddhism by echoing its unique style of evasive language. Yet the *Yogavāsiṣṭha* contradicts Buddhism by insisting upon the primacy of an unchanging self. In its unique form of syncretism, the *Yogavāsiṣṭha* ignores fundamental doctrinal differences by using the reversible blankets of monism and nonessentialism.

I present this digression to highlight the very similar and yet very different approach used by Haribhadra in his examination of Yoga traditions in light of Jainism. Paul Dundas has commented that Haribhadra possessed the "most wide-ranging mind in Jain history," and that his works on Yoga "demonstrate a strikingly liberal approach to alternative, non-Jain attempts to map out spiritual paths."[4] However, while affirming the possibility of both truth and spirituality in non-Jaina Yoga traditions, Haribhadra did not synthesize a new system nor advocate a syncretic approach to coping with the reality of plural religious and philosophical systems. In contrast to the juxtapositional and ambivalent theology of the *Yogavāsiṣṭha*, he honed a carefully charted path that simultaneously and succinctly outlines ways of Yoga theory and practice and then subtly seeks to demonstrate that Jaina metaphysics most fully accounts for the experience of liberation. In the process, he teaches the reader of the *Yogadṛṣṭisamuccya* about the classical Yoga of Patañjali, the Vedānta-like Yoga of Bandhu Bhagavaddatta, the Buddhist Yoga of Bhadanta Bhāskara, and his own systemization of Goddess Yoga, but he remains committed to the stages of the Jaina spiritual path (*guṇasthāna*).

MANY ENLIGHTENMENTS

In the *Yogadṛṣṭisamuccaya*, Haribhadra emphasizes omniscience (*sarvajña*) as the highest state of Yoga, and he equates this state to highest truth (*tattvam uttamam*, *YDS* 101) and liberation. He asserts that the omniscience attained by the Yogi is always the same, though the circumstances of this experience are, by nature, conditioned by the particularity of each individual soul (*YDS* 109–10). Giving an individualistic twist to an old monistic adage, Haribhadra writes, "There could never be a single road to different cities," advancing a plural theory of liberation and the processes by which it is attained (*YDS* 114). Each soul (*jīva*) achieves its ultimate spiritual goal by following its own karmic path, and Haribhadra celebrates the variegation of "disciplines and practices" (*YDS* 114) that can be followed in the process. He goes on to claim that "People differ in various ways due to their desires and so forth. They enjoy various fruits according to differences in their intellectual dispositions, and so forth" (*YDS* 119).

Though Haribhadra acknowledges many paths, he also claims that similar paths are appropriate for the goal of achieving calmness (*śama*), "like the path on the shore of a lake" (*YDS* 128). I find this image particularly interesting, because rather than talking about the shore of the vast ocean, which is seemingly endless and hence evokes monistic images, each lake will have its own unique contours. The experience of releasing karma and calming the mind will be distinguished by the particular karmic peculiarities of the individual person. Because of similarities in the process of the karmic pacification, this experience will share structural similarities that indicate a similar but not an identical path. All who seek liberation face the challenge of controlling and quieting their karmic impulses. However, because of their individual karma, the path followed by each will be distinct, just as one lake differs from another.

Recognizing both a plurality of approach and a singularity of achievement, Haribhadra writes that "the wisdom gained from discipline is singular in essence, though heard of in different ways" (*YDS* 129). Citing both Hindu and Buddhist names for this, he refers to this final goal as "Eternal Śiva, Highest Brahman, Accomplished Soul, Suchness," noting that "the meaning is one in all the various forms" (*YDS* 130). He further characterizes this final state, by which one achieves calmness, as having "no contradiction, free from disturbance, disease, and action, by which one is freed from birth" (*YDS* 131).

Haribhadra advances a pluralistic approach to liberation, maintaining that the experience of liberation will be unique to each soul, and that each soul's approach will be distinct from all others. However, he also claims that the experience, although approached and experienced uniquely by each liberated individual, will nonetheless hold common characteristics, most notably, the gradual extirpation of karma.

THE IMPORTANCE OF SUFFERING IN THE *YOGADṚṢṬISAMUCCAYA*

If liberation is the hallmark that characterizes Indic religions across doctrinal barriers, then its evil twin is the perdurability of suffering (*duḥkha*) for those who remain trapped within the snares of *saṃsāra*. Two passages from Patañjali's *Yoga Sūtra* quintessentially express this aspect of Indian thought:

> *Pariṇāma-tāpa-saṃskāra-duḥkhair guṇa-vṛtti-virodhāc ca duḥkham eva sarvaṃ vivekinaḥ.* (*YS* II:15)
>
> For the discriminating one, all is suffering, due to the conflict of the fluctuations of the *guṇas* and by the suffering due to change, sorrow, and karmic impressions.

> *Heyaṃ duḥkham anāgatam.* (*YS* II:16)
>
> The suffering yet to come is to be avoided.[5]

Like Patañjali and Buddha, Haribhadra asserts that "every existence takes the form of suffering" (*duḥkha-rūpo bhavaḥ sarvaḥ* [*YDS* 47]. He even claims that meritorious action in fact perpetuates suffering, because it is driven by a desire to help others (*YDS* 173) and can leave a residue of attachment.

Haribhadra also uses the term ailment (*vyādhi*) to convey the pervasive nature of suffering. He claims that for a person to be proclaimed "liberated," he or she must in fact have been afflicted (*YDS* 187). He writes:

> Existence, indeed, is a great illness,
> comprised of birth, death, and disease.
> It produces various forms of delusion,
> and causes the sensation of excessive desire
> and so forth. (*YDS* 188)

For Haribhadra, the only cure to the "disease of worldly existence" is to destroy its cause, which is karma.

In the Jaina tradition, suffering arises from the fettering adherence of karmic material to the individual soul. In the *Yogadṛṣṭisamuccaya*, Haribhadra defines the highest form of Yoga as "the destruction of the karma of the body and so forth" (*YDS* 9). Although he only sparingly uses Jaina jargon in this text, he refers to the accumulation of karmic substance (*dravya*) as the cause of agitation (*YDS* 27). Through the destruction of impurity (*bhāvamale kṣīṇe*), one advances toward liberation, which arises with the destruction of marks (*lakṣaṇam*) on the soul (*YDS* 31).

In various places, Haribhadra identifies the source of bondage with karma, and states that "those with excessive sin . . . have been cut down by their own actions" (*YDS* 152). In a critique of the libertine notion that experience can help liberate one from attachment, he writes, "Trying to stop desire through enjoyment is like removing a burden from one shoulder and placing it on the other shoulder. Like that, karmic residue (*saṃskāra*) is created" (*YDS* 161). This critique will be taken up in greater detail in the next chapter. Although these references to karma are not accompanied by detailed descriptions of specific karmic formations (*prakṛti*-s) or any mention of the theory of karmic colors, he clearly advances the position that karmic substance must be purged.

LIBERATION

In Haribhadra's descriptions of liberation in the *Yogadṛṣṭisamuccaya*, he uses a beautiful metaphor, likening the practice of Yoga to cleansing winds that destroy "the clouds of destructive karma." He writes:

> With faults eliminated, omniscient,
> endowed with the fruits of all that can be accomplished,
> with things to be done now only for the sake of others,
> such a one attains the end of Yoga. (*YDS* 185)
>
> Therein the blessed one quickly attains highest *nirvāṇa*
> through the Yoga of total freedom, the best of Yogas,
> having accomplished the cessation
> of the ailment of worldly existence. (*YDS* 186)

By performing Yoga and systematically disengaging from the influence of karma and its residues, one achieves the state of liberation, characterized as faultlessness. Haribhadra emphasizes that the chief ailment of the soul is the process of generating various karmas, and that when this ceases, one "reaches the prime state of liberation" (*YDS* 190).

This procedure does not differ significantly from the philosophy of Yoga put forth by Patañjali. In the *Yoga Sūtras*, the suppression of all karmic residue (*saṃskāra*) leads to a state of liberation known as "seedless (*nirbīja*) *samādhi*" (*YS* I:50, 51). All karmas are said to be afflicted with one or more of the five impurities, listed by Patañjali as ignorance, egotism, attraction, repulsion, and clinging to life (*avidyā, asmitā, rāga, dveṣa,* and *abhiniveśa,* [*YS* II:3–12]). The operations of karma cause sorrow, to be reversed by the practice of Yoga. Karmic propensity (*pariṇāma*) leads to pain; its reversal leads one toward liberation. Patañjali further describes karma as white, black, or mixed, noting that the karma of a Yogi has no color. The practice of Yoga culminates with the diminishment and expulsion of all karmic residue, accompanied by the cessation of afflicted action (*YS* IV:24–30) and the emergence of a state known as "*kaivalyam,*" or "perfect solitude," in which the pure witness (*puruṣa, ātman, citi śakti*) no longer mistakenly identifies itself with the world of change (*prakṛti*).

In the *Yogabindu (YB)*, Haribhadra summarizes the yogic process as follows: "Due to the linking of the self with karma, one is trapped in *saṃsāra*; through disconnection from that, one is indeed liberated" (*YB* 6). In the *Yogabindu,* in particular, he emphasizes the reality of this process, asserting both the reality of the soul and of karma. He writes: "As long as one is in the state of being connected (with karma), then one is not linked with the interior self (*jīva*). This connection is real; this linking has no beginning" (*YB* 10). Through attachment to karma, one establishes and maintains a sense of ego; by severing this connection, one accomplishes liberation (*YB* 13).

CRITIQUE OF BUDDHIST MOMENTARINESS

Haribhadra develops this advocacy of the real and also distinguishes the Jaina position from that of the Buddhists and the Vedāntins. In both the *Yogabindu* and the *Yogadṛṣṭisamuccaya,* he criticizes the Buddhist notion that there is no distinction between *saṃsara* and *nirvaṇa*, dismissing this position as "fantasy" (*YB* 8). This critique is leveled at Nāgārjuna, who proclaims that there is no difference between transcendence and relativity in the *Mūlamādhyamika Kārikā* (XXV:19).[6] In a critique of the Sarvāstivāda Buddhist position, that all things exist in a sequence of moments (*kṣana*) but disappear shortly following their emergence, he writes: "If everything is nonexistent, then everything is in vain" (*YB* 20). In the *Yogadṛṣṭisamuccaya* (193–97), he repeats this argument, also adding that in fact this notion of continuous birth, maturity, decay, and disappearance cloaks an incipient eternalism: "The defender of endless nonexistence would in fact defend the existence of the Self, because, by this argument, there is no resistance to the notion of eternalness." In response to the often-critiqued Buddhist position that no self or essence abides from moment to moment or birth to birth, which he summarizes as "This indeed does not exist [now]; it exists in a different manner," Haribhadra counters that this is contrary to reason, noting that "something that is always being destroyed cannot be posited." Because perception and experience attest to the abiding nature of things, Haribhadra claims that the reality of existence is indisputable. Furthermore, he claims that the position of nonsubstantiality renders the concept of liberation impossible. If suffering is merely momentary, then it does not truly exist. If it does not truly exist, then there can be no incentive to seek spiritual advancement through purification.

CRITIQUE OF VEDĀNTIN MONISM

Haribhadra also challenges the Vedāntin precepts that all reality shares a common ground such as Brahman, and that the true state of the soul dwells perpetually, eternally, in a state of liberation. He posits in the *Yogabindu* that "if the soul is always in a state of isolation, then the nature of the soul is always without change" (*YB* 8). He reiterates the Jaina position that the soul becomes afflicted with karma, that this affliction is real, and that karma must be expelled. Although he is willing to accept the position of Sāṃkhya that the world is real, he is unwilling to accept the unsullied view of spirit implicit in Īśvarakṛṣṇa's *Sāṃkhya Kārikā*. He aligns Jaina Yoga with Sāṃkhya by identifying the soul (*jīva*) with the witness (*puruṣa*), and he uses the epithet from the *Bhagavad Gītā,* "knower of the field" (*ksetrajña*) (*YB*:17). He also sees commonality among the terms ignorance, *prakṛti*, and *karma*, but he does not accept the premise of a unifying absolute or an underlying substratum. "If existence is absolute, then everything is determined" (*YB* 20). This runs counter to the Jaina insistence on individual determination and to the theory of karma.

In the *Yogadṛṣṭisamuccaya,* he uses a similar argument but emphasizes that the concept of path requires gradated, real states of spiritual progress. Recall that in this text, Haribhadra explicates four different systems of Yoga, drawing parallels to the theory of spiritual stages (*guṇasthāna*-s). He writes that "if only a singular essence is proclaimed, then there could never be the two states of life (*viz.*, happiness and misery)" (*YDS* 198). If the monistic argument is followed through to its logical conclusion, then karmic reality is relegated to a nonexistent ontological status. Haribhadra argues that if this is the case, then there is no incentive to improve oneself; karma would hold no consequence. If this were the case, he posits, "all wordly existence would be called eternal; how could there be the possibility of liberation?" (*YDS* 201).

To the illusionist (*māyāvāda*) position that "appearance is not truth" (*YDS* 202), Haribhadra retorts that this is simply not evident from experience. If the argument is made that Yogic knowledge is of a different quality than illusory knowledge, he claims that this in fact reinforces his point; if yogic knowledge is "from a different state" (*YDS* 203), then both this higher state *and* the other lower state must be real.

To summarize and encapsulate his position, Haribhadra returns to the metaphor of illness and cure:

> If an ailment is nonexistent (as per the Vedāntins)
> or is something else (as the Buddhists claim),
> then, according to either precept,
> [a person] is never liberated from ailment.
> If the one in *saṃsāra* is nonexistent
> or is in fact something else,
> then a liberated one is not liberated!
> Just as in the world one whose illness has disappeared
> is determined to be cured,
> so also for the one who has the disease of wordly existence.
> In the *tantras* he is called liberated due to the destruction [of that disease]. (*YDS* 204–206)

By using this medical analogy, Haribhadra declares karma culpable for all human ills, and prescribes its extirpation.

In conclusion, the concept of the real anchors the thought of Haribhadra in his two Sanskrit Yoga texts. Soul, karma, liberation, and path are all deemed non-negotiable aspects of Yogic theory and practice. Like the Sāmkhya and Yoga traditions and slightly at variance with Advaita Vedānta and Sarvāstivāda and Mādhyamika Buddhism, Haribhadra's spiritual vision finds its roots in grappling with the pressing presence of suffering, the cause of which lies in karma. By observing practices of purification, the Yoga aspirant severs the knots of karma, leading to a state of liberation.

This leads us to consider the earlier statements regarding Haribhadra's approach to non-Jaina points of view. On the one hand, in his Yoga texts, Haribhadra celebrates a wide range of spiritual practices. He generates a new list of Goddess Yoga, starting with the Friendly (*Mitrā*) and extending up through the Highest (*Parā*). He affirms the Yoga of Patañjali. He provides the only extant record of two other eightfold systems of Yoga, one attributed to Bandhu Bhagavaddatta, couched in Vedāntic terminology, and the other attibuted to Bhadanta Bhāskara, using a Buddhistic vocabulary. In the *Yogabindu*, he lavishes praise on Buddhism. In the *Yogadṛṣṭisamuccaya*, Haribhadra expresses hesitation over criticizing the views of other people, as we have seen. However, despite this generosity of spirit, this seeming liberality only barely conceals an immovable commitment to the Jaina position. By alluding delicately to the *guṇasthāna* system, advocating the primacy of karma, and defining the liberation experience in starkly individualistic terms, he clearly regards Jainism, as taught by Mahāvīra and developed by Umāsvāti, as the true path toward each individual's liberation. The reality of the world, the reality of suffering due to karma, and the reality of the individual soul collectively serve as the foundation for Haribhadra's interpretation of Jaina philosophy and practice.

CHAPTER FIVE

Purity in Patañjali and Haribhadra

Jainism emphasizes the purification of one's karma through rigorous abstention from tainted, violent behavior as the only path of liberation. Buddhists and Vedāntins alike have characterized Jainas as holding extreme views, and they have developed different theologies and styles of liberative practice. Patañjali attempted to enfold Jaina asceticism within his explication of Yoga, and he gives great emphasis to the importance of purification. However, Patañjali remains simultaneously committed to upholding the Sāṃkhya definition of *kaivalyam,* or consciousness distinct from identity, as the culmination of Yoga practice. Consequently, Patañjali does not emphasize the dispersal of karma as thoroughly as do Jainism's *Ācārāṅga Sūtra*, Umāsvāti, and Haribhadra. As we will see in this chapter, Haribhadra emphasizes the dispersal of karma and the practice of purity over and above the more metaphysical approach of Patañjali. In the process, he acknowledges the lure of the tantric tradition, which recently had gained in popularity, criticizes its practices (though not its intent), and attempts to demonstrate the superiority of the Jaina spiritual path.

Patañjali, I have argued elsewhere, consistently defends the Sāṃkhya philosophical position that maintains the centrality of discerning the distinction between seer and seen as the key to one's liberation.[1] Haribhadra asserts that purity is the central practice of Yoga, in both his philosophical and sociological explications found in the *Yogadṛṣṭisamuccaya.* In this chapter, purity is examined from the perspective of Patañjali's *Yoga Sūtra* and then as found in Haribhadra's *Yogadṛṣṭisamuccaya.*

PURITY IN PATAÑJALI

In Patañjali, the concept of purity or clarity can be found in the terms *prasāda* (clarity, *YS* I:33, 47), *śuci* (pure, *YS* II:5), *śuddha* (pure, *YS* II:20), *śuddhi* (purity, *YS* II:28, II:41, III:35), and *śauca* (*YS* II:32, II:40). The means of attaining clarity can be found in the descriptions of how to pacify and clarify the mind in the first section, or *pāda*. In the second *pāda*, this purity lies in the observance of the *yamas* and *niyamas*, the central, ethical practices for overcoming the effects of negative *saṃskāras*. In the third *pāda*, the highest of the *siddhis* entails the purity of perfect *sattva*, leading to the knowledge of *puruṣa* (*YS* III:35, 55). In the fourth *pāda*, *dharma megha samādhi* brings about the cessation of afflicted action, a state of purity that can be linked to higher awareness (*citi-śakti*). In the first, third, and fourth *pādas*, the discussion of purification hinges on the perception of the distinction between seer and seen, emphasizing dispassion (*vairāgyam*). In contrast, the second *pāda* emphasizes the active restructuring of one's moral and affective behavior, which is seen as being foundational to overcoming the difficulties inherent in afflicted action (*kliṣṭa-karma*).

PURIFICATION AS THE PATH TO LIBERATION

The *yamas,* or restraints, are listed by Patañjali as nonviolence, truthfulness, nonstealing, sexual restraint, and nonpossession: *ahiṃsā, satya, asteya, brahmacarya,* and *aparigraha.* These are defined as the great vows when "not limited by birth, place, time, or circumstance" [*jāti-deśa-kāla-samaya-anavacchināḥ sarva-bhaumāḥ mahāvratam*, *YS* II:31]. By controlling one's impulses as influenced by the *kleśas,* or afflictions, defined by Patañjali as ignorance, egoism, attraction, aversion, and desire for continuity, one develops new habits (*saṃskāras*) that mitigate against negativity, leading one to a greater state of purity. This process directly correlates to the Jaina practice of the vows (*vrata*) and the theory of karmic expurgation.

Purity can be defined as the opposite of the impurities or afflictions. Wisdom would be the antidote for ignorance, and egolessness for ego. Equanimity toward attractive or repulsive things would be the opposite of attraction and aversion. The last of the five, the desire to continue living (*abhiniveśa*), is said to exist even among the wise, and it would be countered with an attitude of surrender. The application of these antidotes to the poisons of afflictions involves a process that directly correlates to the Jaina practice of vows to facilitiate the expurgation (*nirjarā*) of karma.

Patañjali describes this process of reversing negative karmic influences as the "cultivation of opposites" (or *pratipakṣa bhāvana*), and he writes:

> When there is bondage due to discursive thought, the cultivation of the opposites [is prescribed]. Discursive thoughts like violence, etc., whether done, caused, or approved, consisting of lust, anger, or delusion, and whether mild, medium or intense, have as their endless fruits dissatisfaction and ignorance; thus, cultivation of opposites [is prescribed]. (*YS* II:33–34)

Impurity is described in this verse in terms of the Buddhist categories of lust, anger, and delusion, a simplification of Patañjali's earlier explication of five afflictions, or *kleśas*. Purity, in this instance, would be seen as the absence of lust, anger, and delusion.

The first two stages of eightfold Yoga, the restraints (*yamas*) and observances (*niyamas*), provide the mechanism by which the grip of all these impurities may be loosened. Patañjali describes each of them and lists a corresponding benefit:

> 35. When in the presence of one established in nonviolence (*ahiṃsā*), these is abandonment of hostility.
> 36. When established in truthfulness (*satya*), [there is] correspondence between action and fruit.
> 37. When established in nonstealing (*asteya*), [whatever is] present is all jewels.
> 38. When established in sexual restraint (*brahmacarya*), vigor is obtained.

39. When steadfast in nonpossession (*aparigraha*), there is knowledge of "the how" of existence.
40. From purity (*śauca*) arises dislike for one's own body and noncontact with others,
41. as well as purity of being (*sattva*), cheerfulness, one pointedness, mastery of the senses, and fitness for the vision of the self.
42. From contentment (*santoṣa*), unsurpassed happiness is obtained.
43. From austerity (*tapas*) arises the destruction of impurity and the perfection of the body and senses.
44. From self study (*svādhyāya*) [arises] union with the desired deity.
45. Perfection in *samādhi* arises from dedication to Īśvara. (*YS* II:35–45)

Each of these ten disciplines provides new pathways, new habits for the person on the Yoga path. One can readily find positive qualities that arise from the practice of these disciplines in passages from the Upaniṣads, the *Bhagavad Gītā*, the *Yogavāsiṣṭha*, and numerous other texts that describe the enlightened sage. For instance, the *Bhagavad Gītā* states:

With the elimination of desire and hatred,
Even though moving among the objects of the senses,
He who is controlled by the Self,
By self-restraint, attains tranquility. (II:64)[2]

Through one's self-effort, one curbs afflicted tendencies and gains control over one's lower impulses.

In the second *pāda*, Patañjali unambiguously supports the notion that the Yoga path must entail the observance of a strict moral code. Without the observance of the five vows, common to both classical Yoga and Jainsm, the purification deemed essential to spiritual unfolding cannot be realized. In Patañjali, the essentially negative vows or restraints listed in the five *yamas* lead to the positive attributes found in the *niyamas*.

In his eightfold schematic, Patañjali offers no room for ethical compromise. The first two stages, *yama* and *niyama*, provide the foundation for subsequent Yoga practice. As Georg Feuerstein and Jeanine Miller point out in *The Essence of Yoga*, this need not necessarily be seen as a linear progression. In the perfection of *ahiṃsā*, one sees other beings as fundamentally no different than oneself.[3] Such a vision implies the state of *samādhi*. The *Bhagavad Gītā* states: "the wise see no difference between a learned and humble Brahmin, a cow, an elephant, a dog, or even an outcaste" (*BG* V:18). In seeing all things as equal, with the implication following that all things deserve respect, the wise simultaneously practice the discipline of nonviolence and achieve the state of unific vision, or *samādhi*. Spiritual attainment cannot be separated from ethical observances.

ALTERNATE PATHS TO LIBERATION IN THE *YOGA SŪTRA*

This leads us to the topic of the diversity of Yoga paths in Patañjali, and the issue of moral ambiguity. The eightfold path is just one of many avenues offered by Patañjali. In many of the other disciplines or practices he lists, few specifically ethical directives seem evident. For instance, in the first *pāda*, after discussing practice and dispassion, Patañjali cites dedication to Īśvara, breath control, concentration, sorrowless illumination, nonattachment, dream knowledge, and "meditation as desired" as possible ways to achieve Yoga. However, with the exception of the exhortation of the Brahma Vihāra (a Buddhist formula for the cultivation of friendliness, compassion, happiness, and equanimity, listed in *YS* I:33), none of the practices listed in verses I:17 through I:40 includes an inherently moral message. It could well be argued that in the descriptions of levels of *samāpattis* and *samādhis* that follow, the very notion of burning the seeds of karmic residue carries an inherent ethical requirement. This argument could be further developed through a close analysis of the term *prasāda* in I:33 and I:47, which indicates a state of clarity, if not purity. However, the first *pāda* of Patañjali emphasizes the restriction of mental fluctuations (*citta-vṛtti*) and past conditions (*saṃskāra*), with minimal attention given to ethical behavior.

In the third *pāda*, which outlines the attainments of the great yogic powers (*siddhis*), the Yogi perfects an array of abilities, including knowledge of previous births, facility in the *cakras*, and an understanding of the mind. However, with the exception of an abbreviated reference to the Buddhist Brahma Vihāra, also cited in the first *pāda*,[4] Patañjali calls for the need to distinguish between the seer and the seen, stating that "in the sameness of purity between the *sattva* and the *puruṣa*, there is *kaivalyam*" (*YS* III:55), again emphasizing the metaphysical while neglecting the ethical. Although the term purity (*śuddhi*), used to describe the purity of consciousness,[5] implies ethical behavior, he does not specify how this is to be observed.

In the fourth *pāda*, Patañjali discusses in detail the process of karmic dissolution. We see that distancing oneself from karmic identification is put forth as being indicative of the highest state, again with only an implied ethical mandate. Although all karma is said to be fraught with impurity (*YS* II:12), the accomplished practitioner transcends even the positive avenues created by the *yamas* and *niyamas*: "The action of a Yogin is neither white nor black; that of others is threefold (black, white, mixed)" (*YS* IV:7). If in fact the actions of a Yogi require dispassion and the dissolution of any karmic compulsion, then it would be most probable that the actions of a Yogi would be pure, that they would be free from ignorance, egoism, attachment, aversion, hatred, anger, and delusion. However, the emphasis lies on the side of philosophical, analytical rigor, leaving wide open the possibility that as long as one assumes a posture of detachment, one can perform any deed whatsoever. If we look at Krishna's arguments for Karma Yoga in the *Bhagavad Gītā*, and at the various behaviors of even some contemporary Yogic teachers, as documented in Georg Feuerstein's *Holy Madness*, it could be stated that Yogic purity is a matter of one's perspective and intention. Feuerstein even suggests that mystic adepts transcend all conventional rules:

> They play tricks but all the while remain beyond the conventional sphere of good and evil. This at least is the thrust of both mythology and much of mysticism: Reality in its nakedness, whether mythologically pictured or mystically realized, transcends the moral dimension of human experience.[6]

Though the *Yoga Sūtra* does not necessarily reject the moral dimension, it does imply that the highest form of purity lies outside of normal boundaries.

Hence, in Yoga, two approaches to purity can be gleaned. The first requires following a strict moral code as outlined in the Brahma Vihāra, the five restraints (*yama*) and the five observances (*niyama*). The second is metaphysical: distancing one's identity from all activity. The metaphysical approach claims that one's freedom lies in one's perceptions of the difference between consciousness and activity. The ethical approach takes seriously one's relationship with the world and demands corrective action to replace afflicted karma engendered by past action. Patañjali appeals to both the ethical and the metaphysical but unlike Jainism, does not necessarily conflate them.

PURITY IN HARIBHADRA

As we have seen, Patañjali sets forth the importance of both ethics and identification with one's higher nature in his discussion of various styles and forms of Yoga. Haribhadra, similar to Patañjali, supports the notion that one must overcome clinging and distance oneself from worldly concerns. He states that "those desirous of liberation should have no attachment (*asaṅga*) to grasping anywhere" (*YDS* 148). Although he uses the term *asaṅga*, a word used also in the *Bhagavad Gītā*, in the above verse, and in verses 166, 175, and 178, he does not employ the term dispassion (*vairāgyam*), as found in the *Yoga Sūtra*. Nonetheless, Haribhadra clearly sees a need to distance oneself from the attachments associated with karmic accretions to advance on the spiritual path.

Rooted in the Jaina theory of karmic dispersion, Haribhadra emphasizes the purgative nature of the Yoga path. Several different terms are used to convey the key concept of purity or purification. These include *śuddha* (*YDS* 42) (which Jaini relates to transcendental purity), and its variant uses, *saśuddha* (*YDS* 23, 25), *viśuddha* (*YDS* 26, 73, 163), *pariśuddha* (*YDS* 29, 89, 126), and *śubha* (*YDS* 33, 54, 55) (which Jaini relates to mundane purity).[7] Haribhadra emphasizes the importance of purging all obstructive karmas.

Descriptions of enlightenment, or *samādhi*, the culminating stage of Yoga, referred to by Haribhadra as Parā, or the Highest, can be found in verses 179–92. These passages affirm the centrality of purity to this process, which is certainly implied in Patañjali's Yoga but seemingly accorded a lesser status than the metaphysical shift away from identification with mundane activity to the state of pure witnessing. Haribhadra refers to destroying the clouds of destructive karma by the wind of Yoga (*YDS* 184) diminishing one's faults (*YDS* 185), and he explains the liberation process in terms of ridding oneself of the karmic impulses:

> This is the chief [ailment] of the soul:
> giving birth without beginning
> to the cause of various *karmas*.
> All living beings understand this experience. (*YDS* 189)
>
> When liberated from this,
> then one reaches the prime state of liberation.
> From cessation of the fault of birth and so forth,
> one encounters that state of faultlessness. (*YDS* 190)

Separation from karma rather than entry into the state of the pure seer characterizes the Jaina approach to Yoga, clearly preferred by Haribhadra.

In comparing Patañjali and Haribhadra on the issue of purity, one can make the following observations. Patañjali emphasizes the power of consciousness as the highest goal (*citi-śakti*). He describes ascension to this state as a subtilization process, a lightening process that brings one into a state of pure *sattva*. Three of the many avenues he prescribes for this ascent require conscious, determined ethical transformation: the Brahma Vihāra, mentioned in the first and third *pādas*, and the restraints (*yamas*) and observances (*niyamas*), described in detail in the second *pāda*. Furthermore, in his definition of karma and its general linkage to impurity in *pādas* two and four, Patañjali indicates that the highest state (*dharma megha samādhi*) expels all afflicted action. Any subsequent action presumably could be none other than purified action.

In the *Yogadṛṣṭisamuccaya*, Haribhadra affirms a different philosophical approach to Yoga. Rather than beginning with consciousness as his base definition, he, following Jaina philosophy, as found in the *Ācārāṅga Sūtra* and Umāsvāti's *Tattvārtha Sūtra*, asserts that the key to knowledge lies in the purgation and expulsion of all karmic residue. Consequently, from the onset and throughout the text, the emphasis lies on the necessity of the Yogic aspirant to develop practices that support a program of ongoing purification. Unlike Patañjali, who lets his readers infer or perhaps only presume the importance of purity at all levels of Yoga practice, the beginning, the middle, and the end of Haribhadra's system remind the reader of its necessity.

CHAPTER SIX

Haribhadra's Critique of Tantric Yoga

Patañjali most likely composed the *Yoga Sūtras* in the early centuries of the Common Era, perhaps around 200 C.E. Although he includes references to *cakras,* he does not take up a discussion of the broader Tantric tradition, which, according to archaeological evidence, does not bloom until the fifth or sixth century.[1] By the eighth century, Tantric manuals appeared in both Hinduism and Buddhism that prescribe elaborate rituals to expedite the yogic process and entail participation in activities that under normal circumstances would violate both the Buddhist precepts and the Yogic/Jaina vows listed earlier.

In the eighth century, Haribhadra provided a fascinating glimpse of Yoga traditions, presumably current in his lifetime, and he criticizes some of the practices associated with the emerging Tantric tradition. He lived and wrote during a period of Tantra's ascendancy, and he includes in the *Yogadṛṣṭisamuccaya* many rejoinders to key themes of the Tantric tradition. In the process, he shows the close connections among Jainism, Sāṃkhya, Buddhism, and Yoga, all of which might be deemed "*śrāmaṇa,*" or renouncer traditions, and challenges some aspects of Tantra.

In the second stanza of the *Sāṃkhya Kārikā*, Iśvarakṛṣṇa proclaims that the process of sacrifice, so central within the Brahmanical Vedic tradition and in the many rituals of Tantra, proves ineffectual for assuaging the pain of human existence, and that the more reliable means of knowledge (*jñāna*) must be applied. Similarly, in the *Yogadṛṣṭisamuccaya*, Haribhadra emphasizes the pervasiveness of human suffering and states that people seek liberation because of this enduring discomfort (*duḥkha*). Rather than emphasizing knowledge as the means of liberation, Haribhadra, true to his Jaina faith, insists on the purification of one's karma as the means to liberation. However, like Īśvarakṛṣṇa, he directly criticizes elaborate sacrificial ceremonies, particularly in honor of the goddess. Echoing the standard Jaina disdain for such activities, Haribhadra proclaims that the ritual process only helps desires fester.

During the time Haribhadra lived in India, the Tantric schools were proliferating in both Hinduism and Buddhism. Jainism eventually incorporated many Tantric ritual practices,[2] though, as John Cort points out, Jainas made certain that these remained merely symbolic, without the actual use of the banned substances employed in "left-handed Tantra."[3] Archaeological evidence points to a fully developed goddess tradition by the time of Haribhadra, replete with temples, statuary, texts, and paintings. Vidya Dehejia writes:

> The tantric cult of the Yoginīs, one of the lesser-known sects of the form of heterodox worship referred to as Kaula Mārga, appears to have risen to considerable significance in the centuries following A.D. 600. Increasing numbers of followers were attracted to the cult, drawn presumably by the promise of the magical abilities that these goddesses would bestow on their favoured devotees. The orthodox tradition became increasingly aware of the power of this new religious order that was drawing away such large groups of worshippers. Realising that the Yoginīs possessed a certain persistent and magnetic appeal, it decided to incorporate their goddesses at least into the outer fringes of its own tradition.[4]

This, it seems, is what Haribhadra had in mind, with the hope perhaps not of gaining converts from Kula Yoga to Jainism but of retaining adherents within the fold. He employed two strategies to accomplish his purpose. First, he severely criticized their practices in at least three places in the text. Second, his two original "recastings" of yoga practice are done in a distinctly Tantric manner, as we will see, and he bestows some praise on the intent of Tantra.

Haribhadra states that he composed the *Yogadṛṣṭisamuccaya* in an attempt to communicate with those who, in his assessment, had gone spiritually astray. In verse 222, Haribhadra baldly asserts: "The Kula Yogis, who are drunken and more dull than us, might side with our case from hearing this and derive some small benefit." Yet he specifically backs away from the notion that this be presented directly to them, stating that "The wise ones do not give this to those who are unsuitable; Haribhadra says it is not to be given to them out of respect" (*YDS* 226), and that "contempt that is engendered in this case is unfortunate and very little is gained" (*YDS* 227). He clearly does not want to offend the Kula Yogis nor open himself up to criticism by attempting to convert them to his view. Presumably, this would be in violation of the Jaina precept of nonviolence. In the final verse of the text, he takes the prudent path, stating, "This is to be given to the suitable ones who are established by great effort in the law, along with those lofty ones who have abandoned envy for the sake of removing impediments to true blessedness" (*YDS* 228). His refusal to present it to those for whom it was originally intended ensures that he avoids any harm that might arise from confrontation. It also attests to the deeply held convictions that typify the tensions between the two schools. When Haribhadra states that he hopes the Kula Yogis might be swayed by his interpretation, he in fact is giving voice to a covert theme that seems to pervade certain aspects of the text.

The *Devī Purāṇa*, a text that is perhaps roughly contemporaneous with Haribhadra, provides some examples of what he finds objectionable in "misguided" spiritual practices. For instance, the *Padamālā Mantra Vidyā* describes powers that an initiate can gain through the invocation of Cāmuṇḍa, a form of the goddess closely akin to Durgā. Some of these include such accomplishments as being venerated and popular, or the ability to stop rain at will or to become invisible. Others prove to be quite problematic: "By performing rituals in accordance with the tenth mantra, the worshipper can spread epidemic diseases among his or her enemies. . . . By repeated utterance of the fourteenth mantra, killing someone can be accomplished from a distance. . . . The twenty-sixth mantra, repeated properly with proper oblation, enables one to make another insane. . . . With the power achieved from the thirty-first mantra, the *sādhaka* achieves power to burn down a city."[5] Furthermore, this text specifies that blood sacrifices consisting of animal blood and the devotees' own blood are required in the months of Caitra (March 14 to April 13) and Jyaiṣṭha (May 16 to June 15). Clearly these practices are not in keeping with Jaina religiosity and would prove appalling to Haribhadra.

Haribhadra squarely confronts and attempts to refute some of the basic premises of Tantra. Having quoted what appears to be a formula derived from a tantric text, "Through deliverance from the ocean of worldly existence and shattering of the adamantine karmas, one has obtained entirely what is to be known," (*YDS* 66) he then refutes this view, saying that this does not get to the essence of the subtle. He also characterizes such people as licentious (*avedyasaṃvedya*), and he suggests that their goal is illusory (*YDS* 67).[6] He lambastes teachings or methods of worship associated with the violence of some goddess sacrifices:

> 68. Subtle knowledge is obstructed
> by the dirtiness of destructive power.[7]
> From this and in this teaching
> nothing is ever born.
> 69. Therefore, according to the illumination of scripture,
> this wayward perspective
> is not in accordance with the truth.
> Although it resembles a foundation,
> indeed, from it indeed only sin is generated.
> 70. Now from this,
> other than in the higher levels,
> there cetainly is sin,
> due to the fault of karma.
> If one does this at any time, such a thought
> would be like putting one's foot on a hot iron. (*YDS* 68–70)

Haribhadra contrasts *avedyasaṃvedya*, or licentiousness, to *vedyasaṃvedya*, by which one is said to truly be able to destroy obstacles and turn one's thoughts away from "women" (*YDS* 73), which might in fact refer to the goddesses worshipped in the Kula schools. Followers of licentiousness (*avedyasaṃvedya*) are said to "rejoice in existence" and be "greatly agitated by involvement with objects" (*YDS* 75). In the following sequence, Haribhadra spares nothing in his criticism of such people:

76. The lover of worldly existence is vile,
finding pleasure in acquiring things,
wretched, wicked, filled with fear,
deceitful, engaged in undertakings that bear no fruit.
77. Being full of negative transformations,
such an attitude is not pretty.
Even associating with it is invariably
like mixing food with poison.
78. Indeed, because of that
such deluded persons are blind
when it comes to discriminating between right and wrong.
Their ability to see correctly is suppressed.
79. Despite seeing existence as oppressed by birth, death,
old age, disease, infirmity, sorrow, and so forth,
nonetheless, because of delusion,
they do not shrink from it.
80. They always see evil deeds as something to be done,
and do things that ought not be done.
They see pleasure in suffering
as if drawn to scratch a scab.
81. Just as in such itching
there is no thought of the impact on the scab,
so for those ensconced in enjoyment,
there is no abating of desire.
82. They bind themselves,
violent with desire,
always in darkness,
rendered stupid by the dust of their sin,
never considering truth.
83. Having obtained the highest seed of *dharmas*,
among the human realms of karma
they do not strive with even a little sacrifice
on this earth for true action.
84. Like baited meat on a fish hook they are addicted
to vanity, decadent pleasures, and cruel behavior.

Cruel and lethargic, they renounce the true object of desire.
What a pity!
85. Stepping into licentiousness
is the blindness that makes one fall into unhappiness.
This is to be conquered by the great souls
through the Yoga of good company and sacred doctrine.
(*YDS* 76–85)

In another section of the text, Haribhadra explicitly mentions Kula Yogis and their method of liberation. He acknowledges that they have intellect and knowledge, but he claims that they fall short of achieving the calmness that leads to nirvana:

By the Kula Yogis,
these are considered as adjuncts to liberation.
This can be seen from the combination
of texts and [teachings] on power,
and from the fruits of their attachment.
But the taking up of non-deludedness leads to singular purity;
it gives the fruit of *nirvāṇa* quickly
to those travelling with the purpose
of going beyond worldly existence. (*YDS* 125–26)

He implies in these verses that the Kula Yogis do not seek the highest goal but are most interested in fulfilling their desires.

In yet another section of the text, this time at the conclusion of the discussion of Firmness, the fifth view, Haribhadra critiques those who would try to extinguish a desire by attempting to satisfy it:

159. For the wise, wealth does not bring happiness,
because its friend is poverty.
So should it be for the many
extensive enjoyments of the body,
which in the world have sin as their companion.
160. Even enjoyment arising from *dharma*
is worthless for the path of a living being.
Even if it is arising from the best of woods (sandalwood),
it burns and is consumed by fire.
161. Trying to stop desire through enjoyment

is like removing a burden from one shoulder
and placing it on the other shoulder.
Like that, karmic residue (*saṃskāra*) is created.
(*YDS* 159–161)

A well-known aspect of the Kula cult is the practice of the five "Ms," the forbidden enjoyments of fish, meat, wine, fermented grain, and sexual intercourse, in which one indulges during tantric ritual.[8] Haribhadra implies that the pursuit of these can bring only harm.

Toward the end of the text, Haribhadra again makes mention of the Kula Yogis, in conjunction with four groups of yogis assigned slots within a fourfold assessment of Yoga, including two preliminary phases to the previously mentioned eightfold path. He indicates that Kula Yogis have achieved no stage of Yoga. It is only the next group, the Gotravantas, that occupies the slot titled "Wishful" (Icchā) Yoga. This corresponds to the first level of the threefold scheme at the beginning of the text (Haribhadra identifies himself with this group). The Gotravanta Yogis are said to "display no ill will anywhere, think fondly of gurus, gods, and the twice born, are compassionate and modest, possess wisdom and control of the senses" (*YDS* 211). Haribhadra calls the third level "Engaged" (Pravṛtti) Yoga, said to be observed by the Pravṛttacakras. In this phase, one follows the earlier-mentioned Precept (Śāstra) Yoga. The fourth group of yogis, referred to as Avañcaka, or Authentic, Yogis, practices the two disciplines of Firmness (Sthairyam) and Inconceivable Power (Acintya Śakti) Yoga, which will be described in the next chapter, both of which can be equated to Effort (Sāmarthya) Yoga, mentioned by Haribhadra at the beginning of the *Yogadṛṣṭisamuccaya*.

In verses 209 and 222, Haribhadra indicates that he hopes that the Kula Yogis might read this text and be persuaded to enter into the higher forms of Yoga, a position from which he later retreats. But here his disdain for the Kula Yogis cannot be disguised: he refers to them as "drunken and more stupid than us."

And yet despite his criticisms of the Kula Yogis who practice Tantra, Haribhadra uses several devices that can be seen as attempts to "co-opt" the lure of Tantra. He in fact uses the word "Tantra" various times in the text, always in a positive light. In verse 74, he states that the stage known as "*vedyasaṃvedya*" finds its basis in Tantra. In verse 206, he claims that Tantra states that one can be liberated from the "disease of worldly existence." Further evidence of resonance with Tantra is given in his critique of the Sarvāstivādin and Advaita Vedānta schools, described in an earlier chapter. According to Haribhadra, the momentariness of things in Sarvāstivāda and the illusoriness of things in Advaita Vedānta will vitiate the significance of suffering and hence remove any incentive for self-purification. Because both Tantra and Jainism admit to the reality of suffering, and because both advance a doctrine of living liberation, they share a limited form of kinship. And even though Haribhadra objects thoroughly to Tantric practices, he does include Kula Yogis within his sociological survey of Yoga practitioners, indicating that they are a recognizable, if disreputable, organization of Yoga adherents.

Given the common ground between Tantra and Jainism in their emphasis on the reality of suffering and quest for liberation, Haribhadra employs two undeniably explicit devices that would be recognizable to one familiar with or perhaps interested in Tantra, with its array of Yoginīs, emphasis on liberation, and infamous rituals. The first of these is found in the opening section of the work, in his discussion of three types of Yoga: Wishful (Icchā), Precept (Śāstra), and Effort (Sāmarthya). Perhaps it could be argued that these are similar to Patañjali's Kriyā Yoga: Austerity (Tapas), Study (Svādhyāya), and Devotion (Īśvarapraṇidhāna). The middle practice makes for an easy and a direct correlation, but the first and second aspects are really quite dissimilar between the two systems. In Tantra, however, we find a much closer match in the "three cities" of Icchā, Jñāna, and Kriyā.[9] Icchā is the name of a goddess, mentioned in the *Nityāhṛdaya*.[10] The goddess, Ambikā, also identified with the goddess, Rudrāṇī, is said to consist of Icchā, Jñāna, and Kriyā.[11] This triad corresponds directly to that of Haribhadra: Icchā is found in both systems, Jñāna can be seen as a clear parallel with Śāstra, as both entail knowledge and study, and Kriyā can be seen as analogous with Sāmarthya, because action implies effort. The *Śiva-sūtra* (I.13) states that "The Young Umā is called the Icchā-Śakti,"[12] further establishing a link between the goddess tradition and Haribhadra. The *Lalitā-Sahasranāma,* verse 658 refers to this triad as the form of the goddess's energy:

> The energies of desire, wisdom, and action (*icchāśakti-jñānaśakti-kriyāśakti-svarūpinī*): These correspond to her three qualities. The *Samketapaddhati* says, "Desire is her head, wisdom is her trunk, action her feet, thus her body consists of the three energies." The *Vāmakeśvara Tantra* states also . . . "she, O beloved one, is the energy of desire, wisdom, and action."[13]

From the prevalence of this triad, at least in the later literature of Tantra, it seems likely that Haribhadra adopted a popular tantric convention to serve his own purpose in gaining the attention of persons interested in Tantra and Kula Yoga.

Haribhadra's choice of names for his eightfold analysis of Yoga also indicates an overlap with Tantra. Each of these eight names occurs in the feminine gender, and although Patañjali does use the feminine gender to describe several yogic practices (see *YS* I:33, 35, 36, 41, 42, 43, 44, 46, 48), the manner in which their gender stands out in Haribhadra is noteworthy. All except one or two are actually names of goddesses. Three of the names (Tārā, Balā, and Parā) are mentioned in the *Rudrayamālā*, in a list that includes the names of several other *śaktis*.[14] Tārā also is mentioned in verse 20 of the *Lalitā-sahasranāma* and is specifically referred to as a "Jaina deity" in the commentary on verse 149 of that text. Mitrarūpīnī, a close approximation of Mitrā, is mentioned in verse 565 of the *Lalitā-sahasranāma*. Dīprā, though not cited explicitly as an independent goddesss in the texts available to me, finds a close approximation in the term *Diptā*, which is the lead name for a group of five Tantras.[15] The same name, Diptā, is found in the *Devī Purāṇa*, where it appears as number 15 in a list of sixty-four Yoginīs.[16] Sthiti, a name similar to Sthirā, is found in the *Devī Bhāgavatam* amongst a list of sixty-four Yoginīs.[17] Kāntā is mentioned two times in the commentary on the *Lalitā-sahasranāma*, in verses 256 and 329. Likewise, Prabhā is mentioned in verses 393 and 394.

The final name employed by Haribhadra is Parā. It is used frequently in Tantric literature, as the name of the forty-eighth Yoginī in the *Devī Bhāgavatam*[18] and in verses 366, 790, and 809 of the *Lalitā-sahasranāma*. The *Lakṣmī Tantra* refers to Parā as one of the "six lotuses that exist between the eyebrows and the forehead."[19] Sir John Woodroffe writes that "It is Citi-śakti which is called Parā,"[20] reaffirming the link between Patañjali's description of the highest state and the Jaina notion of *kevala*. In fact, *citi-śakti* are the last words to appear in the *Yoga Sūtras* and consequently describe the culmination of Patañjali's Yoga system.

In addition to Haribhadra's appropriation of goddess and goddess-like names to describe the various parts of his Yoga system, the number eight also holds significance within the Tantric tradition. Originally, a standard grouping of seven mother goddesses was found in the early Tantric texts and temples.[21] However, by the time of Haribhadra, this had extended to eight, a number that then reduplicated itself in the form of sixty-four yoginīs. Perhaps the earliest record of this eight-mother tradition is found in the *Agni Purāṇa*, chapters 52 and 146, which has been dated from before the time of Haribhadra,[22] and in the *Kulārṇava Tantra*.[23]

Although these eight goddess-style names do not correlate to goddesses directly associated with Jainism, such as Sarasvatī, Laksmī, Ambikā, Padmavatī, and Jvālamālinī, they do accord with the evolution of the *vidyās*, which are "multi-word invocations that are presided over by female deities and are learnt by initiation and practicing the prescribed *sādhanā*."[24] Haribhadra himself makes mention of the incorporation of these into a group of sixteen goddesses known as *vidyādevīs*,[25] goddesses who bear names that, although not corresponding to the Dṛṣṭis of Yoga, advanced in the *Yogadṛṣṭisamuccaya*, nonetheless follow a pattern wherein "words of feminine gender . . . gradually become goddesses."[26] The use and worship of the *vidyās* in the early phases of Jainism was restricted to the gain of worldly goals. However, as Cort has noted, they advanced by at least the fifth century to a more respectable status in an often-repeated story wherein the king of the Nāgas grants two of his ministers dominion over two groups of eight *vidyās*.[27] One list of eight goddesses found in Mallisenasūri's *Srī Bhairava Padmāvatā Kalpa* discussion of the Pañcaparamesthi Mantra includes the names Jayā, Vijayā, Ajitā, Aparājitā, Jambhā, Mohā, Stambhā, and Sthambhinī.[28] Although none of these names duplicates those used by Haribhadra in the *Yogadṛṣṭisamuccaya*, the tradition of eight goddesses obviously was become well established by the time of thirteenth-century scholar Mallisenasūri.

However, as noted above, the *vidyās* are associated with the fulfillment of worldly desire, in contrast to the role that Haribhadra's eight levels of Yoga play in the advancement toward liberation.

Although it is not possible to determine if any clear precedents exist in Jainism that link the names of Haribhadra's eight levels of Yoga with the Jaina goddess tradition, there seems to be clear evidence that he employed specifically tantric rhetoric in his text to counter and co-opt the tantric traditions such as Kula Yoga. Haribhadra's dismissal of the Buddhist and Vedāntic positions is formulaic and perfunctory, repeating arguments that appear in many other texts. However, his concern about and attention to the Kula Yogis is noteworthy, particularly because he seems to acknowledge a kinship with them, because of their shared perception of suffering (*duḥkha*), and their shared assumption that human effort is the only viable means for release. Unlike the irredeemably antitantric position found in Somadeva's *Yaśastilaka*,[29] Haribhadra seems to hold out hope that some window of convincingness exists to woo the Kulas away from their errant ways. Consequently, in addition to countering what Jainas consider the "extreme positions" of annihilationism and eternalism, he emphasizes the path of purity as the only true yogic means to liberation. However, he attempts this in a subtle fashion. Rather than emphasizing the particular (and stringent) aspects of Jaina purification practice, Haribhadra cloaks the Jaina *guṇasthāna* system in the combined guise of Patañjali's Aṣṭānga Yoga and a Tantric Aṣṭa Mātṛkā system. Some of the names he employs are well known as Hindu goddesses or yoginīs; others are close approximations. Through this device, and by introducing the text with a thinly veiled reference to the threefold emphasis on Desire, Study, and Practice in Tantric traditions, Haribhadra hopes to keep the faithful within the fold by demonstrating that the tantric movements offer nothing other than what already exists in the practice of his form of Jaina Yoga.

CHAPTER SEVEN

Haribhadra's Sociology of Yoga and Its Culmination

One of the fascinating aspects of Haribhadra's *Yogadṛṣṭisamuccaya* lies in its description of different styles of Yoga practiced in eighth-century India. In this chapter we examine his descriptions of these Yogas: Kula, Gotravanta, Pravṛttacakra, and Avañcaka, which can be translated as Family, Clan, Engaged, and Authentic Yoga, respectively. These categories also can be used to describe some of the movements of Yoga that have become popular in the contemporary world. In conclusion, we discuss Haribhadra's description of the culmination of Yoga.

The first reference to a Yoga school can be found in Haribhadra's characterizations of what he refers to as the "Kula" group. This term alludes to the sorts of practitioners that are described in the *Kulārṇava Tantra* and in the works of David Lorentzen, Agehananda Bharati, David Gordon White, Douglas Renfrew Brooks, and other scholars of Tantra. In the prior chapter, we examined how Haribhadra developed a rhetoric designed to convince the followers of Kula Yoga to change their ways, pointing out that although they may have the right intentions, that is, they may truly desire to overcome suffering, they lack the appropriate method for achieving this goal and in fact will only mire themselves in deeper suffering through their misguided practices.

The second group, the Clan Yogis, or Gotravantas, had an insight into the true meaning of Yoga. Presumably, they had the

TABLE 6.1

Four Types of Yogis Mentioned in the *Yogadṛṣṭisamuccaya*

Yoga Group	**Discipline (Yama) Attained**	**Form of Yoga Attained**	**Aṅga Attained (Patañjali)**	**Guṇasthāna Attained**
Family (Kula)	none	none	none	1
Clan (Gotravanta)	Wishful (Icchā)	Wishful (Icchā) Yoga	none	2–4
Engaged (Pravṛttacakra)	Engaged (Pravṛtta)	Precept (Śāstra) Yoga	1	5–7
Authentic I (Avañcaka I)	Firmness (Sthairyam)	Effort (Sāmarthya) Yoga	2–5	8–11
Authentic II (Avañcaka II)	Inconceivable Power (Acintya Śakti)	same	6–8	12–14

[Christopher Key Chapple]

experience of the enlightened view (*samyak-dṛṣṭi*), discussed in the first chapter. They attained the discipline of Wishful Yoga and might be deemed part of the group of Yogis in the *Bhagavad Gītā* that actually tries to practice Yoga.[1] Having had a glimpse of spiritual life, they developed a basic orientation, placing them on the path toward liberation. Haribhadra, as noted earlier, praises this group, stating:

> These [yogins] display no ill will anywhere,
> think fondly of gurus, gods, and the twice born,
> are compassionate and modest,
> and possess wisdom and control of the senses. (*YDS* 211)

This group exhibits the qualities of the first discipline (*yama*), which Haribhadra refers to as "Icchā," the same name as the first of his threefold list of Yogas: Icchā, or Wishful. This also is the Tantric name of the first of the three cities comprising Brahman's manifestation of power (*śakti*) in the manifest world.[2] This concept also corresponds to the first aspect of the threefold Jaina Yoga (*ratnatraya*): right view (*saṃyak darśana*), to be followed by right knowledge (*saṃyak jñāna*) and right action conduct (*saṃyak cāritra*). Haribhadra describes this first phase of Yoga to which he attributes the Gotravantas:

> Wishful Yoga (*icchā*) is spoken of with respect to one who,
> though wishing to practice and knowledgable of the
> meaning of the scriptures, is deficient
> in the Yoga of prescribed conduct (*dharma-yoga*),
> on account of negligence. (*YDS* 3)

Haribhadra characterizes this first stage as an undying willingness to probe into topics of a spiritual nature. He writes that this includes "love of discussion that does not change" (*YDS* 215).

The third group, the Engaged or Pravṛttacakra Yogis, is said to display the first two of Haribhadra's disciplines (*yama*): the Wishful and Engaged (*pravṛtti*) Yogas. This stage of entering into the application of Yoga practices yields an "ubiquitous calm" (*YDS* 216) and would correspond to living according to the Precept, or Śāstra Yoga mentioned in his threefold scheme. He describes Precept Yoga as characterized by "adequate strength and a carefulness born of faith in the advice of those with sharp understanding" (*YDS* 4). Precept Yoga would allow one to fully demonstrate a comprehension and an understanding of performing the ethical restraints or vows, referred to as "Vrata" in Jainism and "Yama" in Patañjali. This would establish one in the first of Patañjali's stages, and in spiritual stages (*guṇasthānas*) five through seven of the Jaina tradition.

The final group described by Haribhadra is the Authentic, or Avañcaka, Yogis. This group of Yoga practitioners has attained the third and highest of his opening threefold scheme: Effort (*sāmarthya*) Yoga. He earlier described this form of Yoga as follows:

> Effort (*sāmarthya*) Yoga is known as the highest Yoga.
> It arises from an abundance of power (*śakti*)
> stemming from the steadfast observance of the precepts.
> It is the dwelling place of the accomplished ones. (*YDS* 5)

This final group is divided into two gradations. The first gradation has attained the third of Haribhadra's four special stages: Firmness (*sthairyam*, not to be confused with the *sthirā*, one of Haribhadra's eight stages). In this, one is clearly ensconced in the path of purification. This attainment can be correlated to the attainment of *guṇasthānas* eight through eleven, the beginning of the unpreceded spiritual stages (*apūrvaka guṇasthānas*). This involves the entry into the Śreṇis, or Ladders, of either Suppression (*upaśama śreṇi*) or Elimination (*kṣapaṇa śreṇi*). As explained in the second chapter, the first ladder culminates in the eleventh *guṇasthāna*, followed by a descent to a lower level and the need to recommence the path. The second ladder leads one to the twelfth *guṇasthāna* and, hence, to the second and highest gradation of this fourth phase. Haribhadra indicates that the first-gradation Authentic Yogis, those who attain Firmness (*sthairyam*), enter into the Ladder of Suppression (*upaśama śreṇi*), and that they rise only to the eleventh *guṇasthāna*.

The highest yoga is described by Haribhadra as the "Yoga of Inconceivable Power" (*acintya śakti*), reminiscent of Patañjali's description of the power of awareness (*citi-śakti*) in the concluding verse of the *Yoga Sūtra*. Haribhadra describes this state as follows:

> The fourth discipline (*yama*) is accomplished
> by the Yoga of Inconceivable Power,
> resulting in the perfection of unsurpassed purity of self
> and goodness for the sake of others. (*YDS* 218)

In this highest form of Yoga, one has entered the Elimination Ladder (*kṣapaṇa śreṇi*) state. This includes the final three *guṇasthānas*: the obliteration of passion with diminished delusion (*kṣīṇamoha*), the obliteration of delusion while retaining connection with the body (*sayoga-kevala*), and the final state of release from all karmic connections (*ayoga-kevala*). Those who have attained this highest state then become an inspiration for all spiritual aspirants. As indicated consistently throughout the Jaina tradition, reflection on and gazing upon the image of the perfected beings (*siddhas, tīrthaṅkaras*) comprise an important aspect of Jaina religiosity.[3] Hence, even though the liberated one no longer maintains any attachment to worldly concerns, she or he becomes an ideal for the emulation of others. Haribhadra addresses the theme of perfection in several verses of the *Yogadṛṣṭisamuccaya*, which will be discussed in the final section of this chapter. However, before pursuing the discussion of the culmination of Yoga, some contemporary analogues for Haribhadra's four types of Yoga groups will be explored.

CONTEMPORARY YOGA

When I first moved to Los Angeles, one spiritual organization operated a bookstore in Santa Monica that had a rather interesting way of grouping its titles. Apparently, its leader had, on several occasions, passed judgment on the depth of insight of several traditions and several individual teachers. The books were arranged accordingly. I found this a bit idiosyncratic, and I was intimidated by the thought of the store clerk sizing me up and directing me to the appropriate level! I offer this story as a cautionary tale: any attempt to pass judgment on the attainment or life state of another individual is fraught with peril. I am reminded of an emphatic statement made to me by a group of devout Jaina laypersons while I visited Jaina Vishva Bharati in Ladnun, India, several years ago: No one can judge your level of spiritual attainment (*guṇasthāna*), because no one can follow you into death. This group also quoted to me a passage from Umāsvāti's *Tattvārtha Sūtra* (10.7) and stated that the uniform that one wears carries no bearing on one's ultimate spiritual attainment.[4] Within this group's tradition, even a layperson can excel within the Jaina path.

Nonetheless, Haribhadra wrote the *Yogadṛṣṭisamuccaya* with the intent of correcting false views and perhaps of winning over the Kula Yogins from their "drunken ways" and onto the path of purification. In my Preface, I mentioned that part of my concern in bringing forth a new translation (however flawed) and interpretation of the *Yogadṛṣṭisamuccaya* was similarly to let Haribhadra's emphatic voice be heard in the context of the practice of contemporary Yoga. On the one hand, I do not want to judge and would prefer to live by the adage "live and let live." However, when misguided notions lead to meaningless suffering, it seems that a small voice is better than no voice at all.

In the world of Yoga today, there exists a wide range of styles of practice and intentions. At many health clubs, Yoga is taught with only one intent: enhancement of one's physicality. In such a context, Yoga generally does not include more than a philosophy of bodily well-being. It would be difficult to characterize this style of Yoga in any of the categories set forth by Haribhadra, unless of course one sees the desire to improve one's body as being within the ambit of reducing the suffering that one experiences due to bodily aches and pains.

At a slightly higher level, one can find particular Yoga teachers who infuse their teachings with an earnest dose of spirituality. In recent years, there has been increased interest in the study of the *Yoga Sūtras* and the dawning of a popular Yoga culture in America that begins to resemble the Precept Yoga advocated by Haribhadra. Whether inspired by Ram Dass's *Be Here Now*, by the inspirational spiritual writings of Paramahamsa Yogananda, or by Christopher Isherwood's and Swami Prabhavananda's *How to Know God*, many practitioners of Yoga at least have been exposed to the foundational worldview that grounds Yoga in spirituality.

At the highest level, Guru Yoga, which involves a process of discipleship and a much deeper level of commitment, can be found. According to the *Yoga Sūtra*, since beginningless time,

Īśvara, the paragon of Yogis who has forever been untouched by karma and its fruitions, has served as an inspiration to pursue the spiritual path. Within Jainism, the model provided by the Tīrthaṅkaras, the Siddhas, the Preceptors, and the community of monks and nuns has offered a clear path for lessening one's karma and advancing toward the state of total spiritual purification.[5] In this style of Yoga, one apprentices oneself to a teacher. If one's intentions are clear, then this relationship can effect significant changes in one's physical, psychological, and spiritual well-being. In some instances, this can be beneficial and wholesome. In other instances, if one's teacher is not well chosen, then the results can be ambiguous, if not potentially disastrous, as in the case of Fred Lenz, cited in the Preface.

Several contemporary Yoga movements and organizations attribute a divine or near-divine status to their leaders. The ideal of a liberated person can be very inspiring. It can, however, lead to abuse and manipulation of followers whose psychological makeup and desire to be parented lead to an unwholesome dependency. Georg Feuerstein, aligning himself with Ken Wilber on this issue, has expressed reservations about "cultic developments" that might occur, "developments that appear to stem directly from an authoritarian style that encourages the totemization of the guru in immature individuals."[6] Many traditions, including the Jaina tradition, solve this potential problem by stating that no one can ultimately save anyone else, and that for over 2,000 years, no one has met the criteria of attaining the fourteenth *guṇasthāna*, that is, total separation at the point of death from all the remaining karmas of life span, name, family, and sensation.[7] Although this might seem a bit dour, it gives one pause to consider that all persons in the human body, even the most elevated, grapple with the living reality of cause and effect in day-to-day life.

How, then, can one develop the moral compass needed to enter into a genuine path of spirituality, referred to by Haribhadra as "Authentic," or Avañcaka Yoga? One has to assume, first, that one agrees to the basic orientation of Yoga, that is, that one's being has become shrouded with the clouds of karmic substance (*dravya*), and that the practices of Yoga will help diminish and eventually remove these coverings (*āvaraṇa*). Second, one has to be willing to shape one's thoughts and actions through the application of ethical precepts. In both Yoga and Jainism, this means taking on a daily commitment to the ideals of nonviolence, truthfulness, not stealing, sexual restraint, and nonpossessiveness. Finally, one needs to hold forth for oneself an ideal spiritual goal. In Yoga, this would involve developing a relationship with an ideal image of the perfected self; or, in Jainism, a commitment to the ideal of liberation set forth by the Jina, the Siddhas, the teachers, and the monks and nuns.

THE CULMINATION OF YOGA

For Haribhadra, the following points are important for an effective spiritual life. Self-effort is essential. Each being holds a perspective on reality that is unique, formed by his or her individual engagement of karma over countless births. Though a teacher may be concerned and interested in a student's well-being, and may establish a context for self-discovery and self-purification, no one has the power to set anyone else free. In the words of my own preceptor, the late Gurāṇi Añjali, "We come alone, and we go alone." The spiritual goal, as framed by Yoga and Jainism, is one of blessed solitude. The task of spiritual advancement is a heroic one, requiring a willingness to live a life of self-examination and self-correction, guided by the ideals of spiritual purity, not conformity to convention.

In Haribhadra, the path can be summarized as an acknowledgment of the reality of suffering coupled with a quest for purity. Haribhadra emphasizes the need to be in touch with the causes and effects of one's fragile humanity. The practices of Yoga may generate feelings of goodwill and even states of bliss. However, to be effective, these experiences also must bring one into a direct perception of the routine, and sometimes unconscious, violations of the precepts listed earlier that perpetuate pain in others as well as in oneself. By careful observation of one's way of being in the world, one can learn to correct the subtle forces that prompt one to be, in the words of Patañjali, ignorant of one's true self, egotistical, attached, repulsed, and fearful of death. This requires diligence, vigilance, and honesty, and the willingess to subject oneself to criticism by others. Ultimately, the only antidote can be found in a commitment to self-purification. According to Gandhi, the salvation of the world begins with the salvation of one's self. As the philosopher, Ortega y Gasset, has stated: "I am my self and my circumstances. In order to save my self, my circumstances must be saved."[8] The human quest for authenticity mandates that one grapple with one's inner impulses to heighten and purify one's relationship with the world.

In the final analysis, Yoga, regardless of the philosophical or theological school through which it is expressed, emphasizes the real possibility of human freedom. Haribhadra attempted to communicate this ideal as a pan-cultural possibility, found within all of the philosophical and religious traditions to which he had access. As a Jaina, Haribhadra held up the notion of total freedom (*ayoga*) as the ultimate goal. He writes that once one enters the Ladder of Elmination stage and systematically disengages from all karmic impulses, one approaches freedom:

> Indeed, on account of this, the Yoga of Total Freedom (*ayoga*)
> is declared the highest of Yogas.
> Characterized by the renunciation of all things,
> it is truly the path of liberation, (*YDS* 11)

Haribhadra employs the metaphor of clouds to describe the nature of karmic obscuration. He writes:

> Like clouds that come and go in the night,
> like the graspings of a small child—
> so indeed is the view of the stream [of worldly
> existence] to be understood.
> Otherwise, one is dwelling in a mistaken view.
> (*YDS* 14)

> In truth, one does not approach great uplift
> within this realm of gross matter.
> How can genuine form be grasped
> when the eye is clouded? (*YDS* 36)

With the various species of karma in a purified state,
the *jīva* becomes established in cool, moonlike radiance.
With respect to this, ordinary consciousness
is like a cloud concealing the moonlight. (*YDS* 183)

It is said that at the time
when the clouds of destructive karma
are themselves destroyed by the wind of Yoga,
that is the escape.
Then the glory of singular knowledge is born. (*YDS* 184)

This brings one to the final state, as defined by Haribhadra:

> With faults eliminated, omniscient,
> endowed with the fruits of all that can be accomplished,
> with things to be done now only for the sake of others,
> such a one attains the end of Yoga. (*YDS* 185)

The culmination of Yoga can be no less than the severance of one's self from all entanglements. Through the process of gradual purification, through the sloughing off of all karmic attachments, and after having subjected oneself to an honest, authentic process of self-examination and self-correction under the guidance of a suitable preceptor, one moves out from behind the clouds and into the gleaming, pure light of awareness.

Forms of Yoga as Given in Haribhadra's *Yogadṛṣṭisamuccaya* and Comparisons

Haribhadra	**Patañjali**	**Bandhu Bhagavaddatta**	**Bhadanta Bhāskara**	**Guṇasthāna**	**Patañjali's Samādhi**
Mitrā (Friendly)	Yama (Disciplines)	Adveṣa (No Aversion)	Akheda (No Distress)	4–7; insight and ethics	*citta-vṛtti*
Tārā (Protector)	Niyama (Observances)	Jijñāsa (Desire for Knowledge)	Anudvega (No Anxiety)	8; in path, with passions	*samāpatti*
Balā (Power)	Āsana (Postures)	Śuśrūṣā (Desirous to Hear Truth)	Akṣepa (No Distraction)	9; with gross passions	*savitarka*
Dīprā (Shining)	Prāṇāyāma (Control of Breath)	Śravaṇa (Hearing Truth)	Anuttānavatī (No Interruption)	10; with subtle passions	*nirvitarka*
Sthirā (Firm)	Pratyāhāra (Detachment)	Sūkṣmabodha (Subtle Awakening)	Abhrānti (Unmuddied)	11; no passion, calmed delusion, no omniscience	*savicāra*
Kāntā (Pleasing)	Dhāraṇā (Concentration)	Mīmāṃsā (Reflection)	Ananyamud (Not Finding Pleasure in Anything Other)	12; no passion, diminished delusion, no omniscience	*nirvicāra*
Prabhā (Radiant)	Dhyāna (Meditation)	Pratipatti (Perception of Truth)	Arug (Without Pain)	13; no passion, no delusion, with body	*sabīja*
Parā (Highest)	Samādhi	Sātmī-kṛta-pravṛtti (Enactment of Absorption)	Saṅga Vivarjitā (Free from Attachment)	14; omniscience, no activity	*nirbīja*

Yogadṛṣṭisamuccaya

(A Collection of Views on Yoga)

HARIBHADRA

Translated by
Christopher Key Chapple
and
John Thomas Casey

A NOTE ON THE TRANSLATION

The *Yogadṛṣṭisamuccaya* is comprised of 228 *ślokas*, a standard verse form that includes thirty-two syllables generally divisible into meaning units of two sixteen-syllable lines, further divided into two eight-syllable units. The verse form dates from before the Christian Era and is employed in the *Rāmāyāṇa* and in the *Mahābhārata*, as well as in Purāṇic literature.

In translating the *Yogadṛṣṭisamuccaya*, we have drawn from two critical editions of the text. These critical editions collate multiple manuscript versions of the text. The earlier edition was published by the Italian Sanskritist Luigi Suali (a student of Hermann Jabcobi) by the Jaina Dharma Prasaraka Sabha in Bhavanagar in 1911. The other (and more reliable) edition was published by the Jaina Grantha Prakashaka Sabha in Ahmedabad in 1940. We have obtained copies of both texts from the L. D. Institute of Indology in Ahmedabad. Both include the so-called autocommentary (*Svopajña*), which although attributed to Haribhadra most likely was either penned by a later author or augmented by later copyists. For various obscure passages, Dr. Yajneshwar Shastri has assisted by giving us alternate readings of the text and has helped us consult passages from Yaśovijaya's *Dvātriṃśaddvātiṃśikā* that discuss the *Yogadṛṣṭisamuccaya*. Samanis Charitra and Sharda Pragya also have graciously read through the text and made suggestions. We also consulted with Dr. Pravin L. Shah and Pandit Dhirajlal Mehta regarding the text.

The *Yogadṛṣṭisamuccaya* was translated previously into English by K. K. Dixit. It is available through the L. D. Institute of Indology in Ahmedabad and includes useful prefatory and interpretative material. We have prepared this new translation for various reasons. Our methodology of translation attempts to retain the "feel" of the original verses. With only rare exceptions, Dixit translates each thirty-two syllable verse as a single sentence. To the extent possible, we have opted for a sparer translation that somewhat preserves the phrasing and rhythm of the original verses. We also have attempted to identify thematic breaks in the text to emphasize Haribhadra's dazzling command of Hindu and Buddhist thought.

The analysis of the *Yogadṛṣṭisamuccaya* in this book includes many important aspects of the text that have not been previously discussed fully, including the relationship between classical Yoga and Jainism and Haribhadra's comparative assessment of different Yoga paths. The prior chapters explored the parallel between the Jaina progressive stages of spirituality (*guṇasthānas*) and the eight stages of the various Yogas described by Haribhadra. Haribhadra's detailed critique of goddess worship and Tantric traditions has been highlighted, as well as the heuristic devices that Harbibhadra used in an attempt to convert his readers to the Jaina view, such as the appropriation of goddesslike names to describe his rendering of Yoga and his praise and "Jainification" of action, scripture, and faith, three key terms used in the Tantric schools, with which Jainism found itself in competition.

While translating, we have tried to direct particular attention to how the author chooses and uses key terms in an attempt to make our translation of these terms consistent. For instance, *ayoga* is a very important technical term in Jainism. It can be translated simply as "disjunction." However, after grappling with this term over a period of several years, we agreed upon the term *total freedom*, which has been applied consistently throughout the work, signalling the importance of this key idea. Similarly, after much anguish and consultation with several scholars, we decided to translate the term *avedyasaṃvedya* as "licentiousness."

Although the text includes what is described as an "autocommentary," K. K. Dixit indicates that he regards it to be written by someone other than Haribhadra. He notes that "at some places it seemed that the commentator has misunderstood the text."[1] In our work, we have learned to become suspicious of commentaries.[2] At times, commentators neglect to trace terms used throughout the text and often fail to see continuity in the main author's style or vocabulary. Furthermore, we have learned that subsequent commentators parrot their predecessors and fail to offer new insights. For example, Dixit states that he follows the commentary because Yaśovijaya has done so.[3] Consequently, we have challenged the commentary but have provided a rationale for doing so, most notably, as indicated in chapter five, regarding the term *avedyasaṃvedya*, which, as noted above, we decided to translate as "licentiousness" and not as "outer limbs," or *bahiranga,* as suggested by S. M. Desai.[4]

Wherever possible, our rendering of the Sanskrit attempts to reflect the sense of completeness and symmetry innate to the *śloka* style. In cases where meaning can only be conveyed through the use of an additional word or two, we have indicated any supplements with brackets and explanatory terms with parentheses. We apologize for any errors, and we welcome the day when yet another translation of this fascinating text will appear.

The *Yogadṛṣṭisamuccaya* of Haribhadra

BENEDICTION

natvecchāyogato'yogaṃ yogigamyaṃ jinottamam
viraṃ vakṣye samāsena yogaṃ taddṛṣṭibhedataḥ

1. Having bowed to Mahāvira,
known by *yogins* as the Supreme Victor,
I will concisely discuss Yoga from a variety of perspectives,
from Wishful Yoga to the level of Total Freedom (*ayoga*).

THREE TYPES OF YOGA (VERSES 2–8)

ihaivecchādiyogānāṃ svarūpam abhidhiyate
yogināṃ upakārāya vyaktaṃ yogaprasaṅgataḥ

2. Since this is certainly an opportunity
for Yoga to be presented for the benefit of yogins,
the character of Yogas will be described,
beginning with the Wishful.

kartum iccoḥ śrutārthasya jñānino'pi pramādataḥ
vikalo dharmayogo yaḥ sa icchāyoga ucyate

3. Wishful Yoga (*icchā-yoga*) is spoken of with respect to one who,
though wishing to practice and be knowledgeable of the meaning of the scriptures,
is deficient in the Yoga of prescribed conduct (*dharma-yoga*),
on account of negligence.

śāstrayogas tv iha jñeyo yathāśakty apramādinaḥ
śrāddhasya tīvrabodhena vacasā'vikalas tathā

4. Precept (*śāstra*) Yoga is known
when there is adequate strength
and a carefulness born of faith
in the advice of those with sharp understanding.

śāstrasaṃdarśitopāyas tadatikrāntagocaraḥ
śaktyudrekād viśeṣeṇa sāmarthyākhyo'yam uttamaḥ

5. Effort (*sāmarthya*) Yoga is known as the highest Yoga.
It arises from an abundance of power (*śakti*)
stemming from the steadfast observance of precepts.
It is the dwelling place of the accomplished ones.

siddhākhyapadasaṃprāptihetubhedā na tattvataḥ
śāstrād evāvagamyante sarvathaiveha yogibhiḥ

6. Herein, the distinctive causes of attainment
of the stage called "Accomplished One"
are certainly not obtained by *yogins*
on the basis of metaphysical texts alone.

sarvathā tatparicchedāt sākṣātkāritvayogataḥ
tatsarvajñātvasaṃsiddhes tadā siddhipadāptitaḥ

7. The reason perfection is acquired in steps
is because the perfection of omniscience
depends on the Yoga of direct realization,
which depends on thoroughly precise discrimination.

na caitad evaṃ yat tasmāt prātibhajñānasaṅgataḥ
sāmarthyayogo'vācyo'sti sarvajñatvādisādhanam

8. And since this is something
which is linked to intuitive knowledge,
it is therefore not inappropriate to say
that Effort Yoga is the *sādhana* (means of achievement)
of omniscience, and so forth.

SUMMARY OF JAINA YOGA (VERSES 9–11)

dvidhāyaṃ dharmasaṃnyāsa-yogasaṃnyāsasaṃjñitaḥ
kṣāyopaśamikā dharmāyogāḥ kāyādikarma tu

9. There are two types of these:
renunciation of *dharma* and renunciation of (all) connections (*yoga*).
While *dharma* (renunciation) stops the desire to be active,
total freedom (*ayoga*) stops the *karma* of the body, and so forth.

This somewhat cryptic verse refers to the fourteen steps of spiritual ascent as outlined by Umāsvāti in his *Tattvārtha Sūtra* described in chapter two. The first thirteen stages, referred to by Haribhadra as "steps," gradually reduce the deleterious conditioning built up over countless lifetimes, propelling the individual soul (*jīva*) to repeatedly take on new births. If one takes up the pursuit of spiritual practice (*sādhana*), then these impulses, referred to as *dharmas*, diminish over time. Ultimately, one transcends even the attachment to name and form, resulting in a disconnection from all materiality known as *ayoga*, or total freedom.

dvitīyāpūrvakaraṇe prathamas tāttviko bhavet
āyojyakaraṇād ūrdhvaṃ dvitīya iti tadvidaḥ

10. The first would be involved with the essences of things,
while the second brings about unprecedented experience.
According to those who know, the second (Yogic renunciation) is higher,
because it releases one from all action.

This verse indicates the distinction between the preliminary phases of spiritual practice and the more advanced phases. In the former, *karmas* remain intact. This would include *guṇasthānas* four through seven: insight (*samyag-dṛṣṭi*), vow taking (*deśa-virata*), complete self-restraint (*sarva-virata*), and higher self-restraint leading to mediation (*apramatta-virata*).[5] In the eighth stage, *karma* begins to actually diminish if one enters the right path. In the eighth *guṇasthāna* of unprecedented experience (*apūrvakaraṇa*), one can enter either the Suppression Ladder (*upaśrama śreṇi*) or the Elimination Ladder (*kṣapana śreṇi*) stage. If one enters the former, one can proceed to the eleventh *guṇasthāna* but will then fall again to the sixth, fifth, fourth, or second stage. If one enters the latter, one skips from the tenth to the twelvth *guṇasthāna* and may proceed higher.[6] By contrasting the terms *dharma*-renunciation and *yoga*-renunciation, Haribhadra indicates that the preliminary form of *dharma*-renunciation establishes habits that will inform future actions; in *yoga*-renunciation, one gradually ceases to be impelled by *karma* in any way, up until the fourteenth *guṇasthāna*, wherein one reaches total freedom.

atas tv ayogo yogānāṃ yogaḥ para udāhṛtaḥ
mokṣayojanabhāvena sarvasaṃnyāsalakṣaṇaḥ

11. Indeed, on account of this, the Yoga of total freedom (*ayoga*)
is declared the highest of Yogas.
Characterized by the renunciation of all things,
it is truly the path of liberation.

A GENERAL ACCOUNT OF THE EIGHT YOGA-DṚṢṬIS (VERSES 12–20)

etat trayam anāśritya viśeṣeṇaitadudbhavāḥ
yogadṛṣṭaya ucyanta aṣṭau sāmānyatas tu tāḥ

12. These three Yogas [Wishful (*icchā*), Precept (*śāstra*), and Effort (*sāmarthya*)]
arise independently on the basis of their distinctions.
The views of Yoga to be spoken of now
are generally recognized as eightfold.

mitrā tārā balā dīprā sthirā kāntā prabhā parā
nāmāni yogadṛṣṭīnāṃ lakṣaṇaṃ ca nibodhata

13. Friendly (Mitrā), Protector (Tārā), Power (Balā), Shining (Diprā), Firm Sthirā), Pleasing (Kāntā), Radiant (Prabhā), and Highest (Parā)
are the names of the Yoga views.
Listen to their characteristics:

sameghāmegharātryādau sagrahādyarbhakādivat
oghadṛṣṭir iha jñeyā mithyādṛṣṭītarāśrayā

14. Like clouds that come and go in the night,
like the graspings of a small child—

so indeed is the view of the stream [of wordly existence] to be understood.
Otherwise one is dwelling in a mistaken view.

tṛṇagomayakāṣṭhāgnikaṇadīpaprabhopamā
ratnatārārkacandrābhā saddṛṣṭer dṛṣṭir aṣṭadhā

15. There is a progressive eightfold view of true perspective which can be compared to
the light of small fires of grass, cow dung, wood, and a lamp,
and with the radiance of a jewel, a star, a flash of lightning, and the moon.

yamādiyogayuktānāṃ khedādiparihārataḥ
adveṣādiguṇasthānaṃ krameṇaiṣā satāṃ matā

16. The Yoga of those engaged in restraint, and so on,
with respect to the abandonment of affliction, and so on,
is thought of by the wise in terms of stages,
[like] the *guṇasthānas* of non-malevolence, and so on.

sacchraddhāsaṅgato bodho dṛṣṭir ity abhidhīyate
asatpravṛttivyāghātāt satpravṛttipadāvahaḥ

17. Bringing about positive (*sat*) activity
by battling negative (*asat*) activity
is considered an awakened view.
From this, one is joined to true faith.

iyaṃ cāvaraṇāpāyabhedād aṣṭavidhā smṛtā
sāmānyena viśeṣās tu bhūyāṃsaḥ sūkṣmabhedataḥ

18. This path may be thought of in eight ways,
according to its diverse ways of uncovering the veil [of ignorance].
But these are only generic distinctions,
as there are numerous others based on subtle differences.

pratipātayutāś cādyāś catasro nottarās tathā
sāpāyā api caitās tatpratipātema netarāḥ

19. The first four are associated with backsliding,
while the higher ones are not.

[The latter four] are able to remove [the veil],
but the others are not, as they [harbor the potential] of backsliding.[7]

prayāṇabhaṅgābhāvena niśi svāpasamaḥ punaḥ
vighāto divyabhāvataś caraṇasyopajāyate

20. On the other hand,
progress without interruption
is like a dream in the night.
Obstacles are overcome through spiritual conduct.

MITRĀ (FRIENDLY) YOGA (VERSES 21–40)

mitrāyāṃ darśanaṃ mandaṃ yama icchādikas tathā
akhedo devakāryādāv adveṣaś cāparatra tu

21. The viewpoint of Mitrā (Friendly) is for the sluggish.
Hence, it advocates restraint of desire and so forth [Patañjali],
being tireless in religious matters [Bhadanta Bhāskara], and,
in another place, it is called "free from malevolence" [Bandhu Bhagavaddatta].

karoti yogabijānām upādānam ihasthitaḥ
avandhyamokṣahetūnām iti yogavido viduḥ

22. The one established here
acquires the seeds of Yoga.
Knowledge of Yoga is considered
the cause that produces liberation.

jineṣu kuśalaṃ cittaṃ tannamaskāra eva ca
praṇāmādi ca saṃśuddhaṃ yogabījam anuttamam

23. Truly, the most excellent seed of Yoga
is a wholesome mind, completely purified,
which offers homage, prostrations, and so forth,
to the Jinas.

carame pudgalāvarte tathābhavyatvapākataḥ
saṃśuddham etan niyamān nānyadāpīti tadvidaḥ

24. Knowing that, there results this excellence
in an individual's last round [of incarnate existence]:

one who is completely purified through these observances
is not [born] another time.

upādeyadhiyātyantaṃ saṃjñāviṣkambhaṇānvitam
phalābhisandhirahitaṃ saṃśuddhaṃ hy etad īdṛśam

25. Perfect devotion is to be followed,
accompanied by the act of curbing conceptual activity.
It is improper to have as one's intention the fruits of such actions.
For then one is indeed endowed with purity.

ācāryādiṣv api hy etad viśuddhaṃ bhāvayogiṣu
vaiyāhṛttyaṃ ca vidhivacchuddhāśayaviśeṣataḥ

26. This [devotion] is to be directed especially to teachers and the like.
In such *yogins* arises a state of purity.
Also, business is to be conducted according to the rules,
so that one has a particularly clear conscience.

bhavodvegaś ca sahajo dravyābhigrahapālanam
tathā siddhāntam āśritya vidhinā lekhanādi ca

27. Nevertheless, agitation naturally comes into being,
nourished by the tenacious grip of karmic substance.
Thus one should resort to the final aim
through following the injunctions, books, and so forth.

lekhanā pūjanā dānaṃ śravaṇaṃ vācanodgrahaḥ
prakāśanātha svādhyāyaś cintanā bhāvaneti ca

28. Therefore, it is said that through books, worship,
giving, listening, and speaking, one is uplifted,
as well as through teaching, study,
reflection, and meditation.

bījaśrutau ca saṃvegāt pratipattiḥ sthirāśayā
tadupādeyabhāvaś ca pariśuddho mahodayaḥ

29. Upon hearing these seed principles
with a firm mental disposition,

there arises an ascertainment born of intensity.
That purified state leads to final emancipation.

etadbhāvamale kṣīṇe prabhūte jāyate nṛṇām
karoty avyaktacaitanyo mahatkāryaṃ na yat kvacit

30. Among these people arises
a noble waning of impurity.
One of undeveloped consciousness
accomplishes nothing of great importance.

carame pudgalāvarte kṣayaś cāsyopajāyate[8]
jīvānāṃ lakṣaṇaṃ tatra yata etad udāhṛtam

31. In finishing up
during an individual's last round,
there arises a species of souls,
concerning which the following is declared:

duḥkhiteṣu dayātyantam adveṣo guṇavatsu ca
aucityāt sevanaṃ caiva sarvatraivāviśeṣataḥ

32. Boundless compassion toward the afflicted,
non-malevolence toward those with noble qualities,
and fitness for service,
in all circumstances, without exception.

evaṃvidhasya jīvasya bhadramūrter mahātmanaḥ
śubho nimittasaṃyogo jāyate'vañcakodayāt

33. So for a great-souled one
bearing the auspicious embodiment of a life of kindness,
there is born a virtuous conjunction of effective circumstances,
due to the development of authenticity.

yogakriyāphalākhyaṃ yac chrūyate'vañcakatrayam
sādhūn āśritya paramam iṣulakṣyakriyopamam

34. Yoga, action, and its fruits
are said to be the threefold authenticity.
Obtaining a most excellent refuge among the holy ones
is like an arrow that finds its target.

etac ca satpraṇāmādinimittaṃ samaye sthitam
asya hetuś ca paramas tathābhāvamalālpatā

35. These, along with respect for the truth and so on,
are the effective circumstances for abiding in the moment.
Thus being with diminished impurities
is the primary cause of this superior state.

Samaya, translated here as "moment," is a Jaina technical term for the smallest unit of time. In the context of yogic practice, bringing the focus of attention to the immediacy of the present moment is a fundamental aspect of the process of achieving liberation from past conditioning and future expectations. The importance of one-pointed, momentary awareness is similarly stressed in Patañjali's *Yoga Sūtra* III.9–12.

nāsmin ghane yataḥ satsu tatpratītir mahodayā
kiṃ samyag rūpam ādatte kadācid mandalocanaḥ

36. In truth, one does not approach great uplift
within this realm of gross matter.
How can genuine form be grasped
when the eye is clouded?

Ghana, translated here as "gross matter," refers to the practice of *karmic* dust that are expelled in the course of Jaina path. Therein, spiritual liberation is seen as a disengagement of spirit from materiality.

alpavyādhir yathā loke tadvikārair na bādhyate
ceṣṭate ceṣṭasiddhyarthaṃ vṛttyaivāyaṃ tathā hite

37. Just as one is not stopped in the world
by the agitation inflicted by a minor illness
and is propelled onward for the sake of obtaining one's desires,
so it is also with this thought once set in motion.

This verse has a double meaning. On the one hand, Haribhadra is using the "struggle" metaphor as encouragement to persevere on the Jaina path of purification. At the same time, he seems to be warning the reader of the tenacity of *karmic* materiality.

yathāpravṛttikaraṇe carame'lpamalatvataḥ
āsannagranthibhedasya samastaṃ jāyate hy adaḥ

38. All of this happens
in the final stage of activity,
since there is little impurity
as one comes close to severing the knot.

Granthi-bheda literally refers to undoing the bonds of *karma*, untying the knot, and releasing the *karmic* material from its deleterious adherence to the individual soul, or *jīva*.

apūrvāsannabhāvena vyabhicāraviyogataḥ
tattvato'pūrvam evedam iti yogavido viduḥ

39. Owing to the absence of deviant behavior,
the "unprecedented" is truly near.
According to a wise one who knows Yoga,
this is indeed of the very essence of the unprecedented.

Apūrva refers to the eighth *guṇasthāna*, which is the beginning of the *śreṇi*, or pathway of highest spiritual achievement.

prathamāṃ yad guṇasthānaṃ sāmānyenopavarṇitam
asyāṃ tu tadavasthāyāṃ mukhyam anvarthayogataḥ

40. What is commonly described as the first stage
is this beginning state,
in accordance with the meaning of Yoga.
[In our reading of the text, this includes the first seven *gunasthānas*.]

TĀRĀ (PROTECTOR) YOGA (VERSES 41–48)

tārāyāṃ tu manāk spaṣṭaṃ niyamaś ca tathāvidhaḥ
anudvego hitārambhe jijñāsā tattvagocarā

41. In Tārā (Protector), it is somewhat clear that
there are the observances (*niyamas*), as already described [Patañjali].

There is freedom from anxiety in setting up undertakings [Bhadanta Bhāskara],
and the field of one's reality is desirous of knowledge [Bandhu Bhagavaddatta].

bhavaty asyāṃ tathā'cchinnā prītir yogakathāsv alam
śuddhayogeṣu niyamād bahumānaś ca yogiṣu

42. So thus, in this stage, there is uninterrupted joy
simply in discussions about Yoga.
On account of the observances of the Yogas of purity,
*yogin*s are held in high esteem.

yathāśakty upacāraś ca yogavṛddhiphalapradaḥ
yogināṃ niyamād eva tadanugrahadhīyutaḥ

43. When there is the power of doing service,
the reward of Yoga increases.
Indeed, from the observances of the *yogins*,
one is connected to that sort of reflection that promotes goodness.

lābhāntaraphalaś cāsya śraddhāyukto hitodayaḥ
kṣudropadravahāniś ca śiṣṭasammatatā tathā

44. And there are other fruits enjoyed in this stage.
Yoked in faith and rising in wholesomeness,
minor misfortunes are diminished,
and one is respected by the learned.

bhayaṃ nātīva bhavajaṃ kṛtyahānir na cocite
tathānābhogato'py uccair na cāpy anucitakriyā

45. Great fear does not arise
and there is no abandonment of what should be done.
Even when neglectful,
these lofty ones do no improper action.

kṛtye'dhike'dhikagate jijñāsā lālasānvitā
tulye nije tu vikale saṃtrāso dveṣavarjitaḥ

46. Situated in excellence and excellent in performance,
one is accompanied by an eager longing, desirous of knowledge.

As if it were innate, one's fear is dispelled,
and hatred is abandoned.

duḥkharūpo bhavaḥ sarva ucchedo'sya kutaḥ kathaṃ
citrā satāṃ pravṛttiś ca sāśeṣā jñāyate katham

47. Every existence takes the form of suffering.
How and when can this be stopped?
This torturous round of existences—
how is this known perfectly?

nāsmākaṃ mahatī prajñā sumahān śāstravistaraḥ
śiṣṭāḥ pramāṇam iha tad ity asyāṃ manyate sadā

48. "Our insight is not great.
The range of *śāstra* (texts) is profound.
The learned are indeed the authorities on this."
One constantly reflects upon these.

BALĀ (POWER) YOGA (VERSES 49–56)

sukhāsanasamāyuktaṃ balāyāṃ darśanaṃ dṛḍham
parā ca tattvaśuśrūṣā na kṣepo yogagocaraḥ

49. When firm within the stage called Balā (Power),
one is prepared for comfortable posture [Patañjali]
and is exceptionally desirous to hear about the truth [Bandhu Bhagavaddatta].
This field of Yoga has no distraction [Badhanta Bhāskara].

nāsyāṃ satyām asattṛṣṇā prakṛtyaiva pravartate
tadabhāvāc ca sarvatra sthitam eva sukhāsanam

50. There truly being no desire at this stage,
even the various species of *karma* are inoperative,
and, in the absence of that,
there is only abiding in comfortable posture.

atvarāpūrvakaṃ sarvaṃ gamanaṃ kṛtyam eva vā
praṇidhānasamāyuktam apāyaparihārataḥ

51. Unlike before, there is no hastiness
in all of one's goings and activities.

One is committed to devotion
and avoids things perishable.

kāntakāntāsametasya divyageyaśrutau yathā
yūno bhavati śuśrūṣā tathā'syāṃ tattvagocarā

52. Just as when a lover and his beloved are joined together,
heavenly songs are heard,
so the united one is desirous of hearing
about this field of reality (*tattva*).

bodhāmbhaḥsrotasaś caiṣā sirātulyā satāṃ matā
abhāve'syāḥ śrutaṃ vyartham asirāvanikūpavat

53. Know that the thought of truth
is like a flowing river, in the absence of which,
instruction is as useless as a well filled with dirt.

śrutābhāve'pi bhāve'syāḥ śubhabhāvapravṛttitaḥ
phalaṃ karmakṣayākhyaṃ syāt parabodhanibandhanam

54. Holding fast to an awareness of the ultimate,
it is said that the destruction of the fruits of action may come about
through the cultivation of a state of purity
whether in the presence or absence of scripture.

śubhayogasamārambhe na kṣepo'syām kadācana
upāyakauśalaṃ cāpi cāru tadviṣayaṃ bhavet

55. In undertaking this Yoga of purification,
there is never any vacillation.
And, indeed, the path of purity
would be the beloved (object) sphere.

pariṣkāragataḥ prāyo vighāto'pi na vidyate
avighātaś ca sāvadyaparihārān mahodayaḥ

56. For one who has gone forth
on this path of self-discipline,

obstacles are not known.
This absence of obstacles,
due to a shunning of objectionable things,
is liberation.

DĪPRĀ (SHINING) YOGA (VERSES 57–64)

prāṇāyāmavatī dīprā na yogotthānavaty alam
tattvaśravaṇasaṃyuktā sūkṣmabodhavivarjitā

57. Dīprā (Shining) is associated with breath control (Patañjali).
This Yoga must not be interrupted even a little [Bhadanta Bhāskara].
One connects with hearing about the true nature of things [Bandhu Bhagavaddatta],
[otherwise] one is deprived of subtle knowledge.

prāṇebhyo'pi gurur dharmaḥ satyām asyām asaṃśayam
prāṇāṃs tyajati dharmārthaṃ na dharmaṃ prāṇasaṅkaṭe

58. The teacher and the *dharma*
are even [more important] than one's life.
Of this truth there is no doubt.
For the sake of *dharma* one will give up one's life
rather than endanger the life of the *dharma*.

eka eva suhṛd dharmo mṛtam apy anuyāti yaḥ
śarīreṇa samaṃ nāśaṃ sarvam anyat tu gacchati

59. There is only one good friend, *dharma*,
who follows one at the time of death.
Everything else goes with the body
at the time of death.

itthaṃ sadāśayopetas tattvaśravaṇatatparaḥ
prāṇebhyaḥ paramaṃ dharmaṃ balād eva prapadyate

60. Thus one who has arrived at that abode,
always hearing those highest teachings,
goes forward from strength of breaths,
indeed, to the highest *dharma*.

kṣārāmbhas tyāgato yadvan madhurodakayogataḥ
bījaṃ praroham ādhatte tadvat tattvaśruter naraḥ

61. Just as a sprouting seed
when placed in salty water is cast away
but in fresh water flourishes,
so also it is with a person who listens to truth.

kṣārāmbhastulya iha ca bhavayogo'khilo mataḥ
madhurodakayogena samā tattvaśrutis tathā

62. Indeed, a mind completely joined
to worldly existence is like salty water,
while hearing of reality
is like joining with fresh water.

atas tu niyamād eva kalyāṇam akhilaṃ nṛṇām
gurubhaktisukhopetaṃ lokadvayahitāvaham

63. Hence, it is due to observances alone
that people become completely wholesome.
One who has become well established in devotion to the *guru*
brings benefit to the two worlds (i.e., the here and the hereafter).

gurubhaktiprabhāvena tirthakṛddarśanaṃ matam
samāpattyādibhedena nirvāṇaikanibandhanam

64. Through the power of *guru* devotion
the vision of *tīrthaṅkara* [ford makers] is seen.
Through forms of meditation and so forth,
one holds hast to *nirvāṇa*.

samyagghetvādibhedena loke yas tattvanirṇayaḥ
vedyasaṃvedyapadataḥ sūkṣmabodhaḥ sa ucyate

65. In this world one who has arrived at the truth
through discrimination of true causes, and so forth,
is said to possess subtle understanding
from knowing what is to be known.

A CRITIQUE OF TANTRA (VERSES 66–85)

bhavāmbhodhisamuttārāt karmavajravibhedataḥ
jñeyavyāpteś ca kārtsnyena sūkṣmatvaṃ nāyam atra tu

66. "Through deliverance from the ocean of worldly existence
and shattering of the adamantine karmas,
one has obtained entirely what is it to be known."
Still, this is not the essence of the subtle in its entirety.

avedyasaṃvedyapadaṃ yasmād āsu tatholbaṇam
pakṣicchāyājalacarapravṛttyābham ataḥ param

67. Those who step into licentiousness
are of excessive manner. Because of this,
the ultimate [for them] resembles the flickering of a bird's shadow
moving across the water.

apāyaśaktimālinyaṃ sūkṣmabodhavibandhakṛt
naitadvato'yaṃ tattattve kadācid upajāyate

68. Subtle knowledge is obstructed
by the dirtiness of destructive power.
From this and in this teaching,
nothing is ever born.

The first Sanskrit compound of this *śloka* is cleverly complex. First, the Sanskrit term *śakti* means "power" and also serves as a generic term for the creative power and essence of the Goddess, in all of her forms. Hindu tantric cults were most often centered around a specific goddess in her tantric manifestation. *Apāya* can mean "wayward," "seductive," or "destructive." The term *mālinyam* is being translated here as "dirtiness," but its use by Haribhadra in this critique of tantric practice is intentionally suggestive of the term *mālinī*. *Mālinī* literally refers to one who wears a garland, but it also is an epithet for the tantric goddess, Durgā. The phrase *apāyaśaktimālinyam* could well be translated as "a garland of destructive power," which is suggestive of the image of Kālī, another important tantric goddess. Thus in a single phrase, Haribhadra critiques the "left-handed" tantric practices that involve sex or the taking of life while simultaneously making thinly veiled references to two of the more important tantric goddesses.

apāyadarśanaṃ tasmāc chrutadīpān na tāttvikam
tadābhālambanaṃ tv asya tathā pāpe pravṛttitaḥ

69. Therefore, according to the illumination of scripture,
this wayward perspective is not in accordance with the truth.
Although it resembles a foundation,
indeed, from it only sin is generated.

ato'nyad uttarāsv asmāt pāpe karmāgaso'pi hi
taptalohapadanyāsatulyā vṛttiḥ kvacid yadi

70. Now from this,
other than in the higher levels,
there certainly is sin,
due to the fault of karma.
If one does this at any time, such a thought
would be like putting one's foot on a hot iron.

vedyasaṃvedyapadataḥ saṃvegātiśayād iti
caramaiva bhavaty eṣā punar durgatyayogataḥ

71. From stepping into that which is sanctioned
arises intense preeminence.
It is said that this, indeed, is the ultimate,
not connecting again with distress.

Again, within this critique of the tantric path, Haribhadra makes a thinly veiled reference to the important tantric goddess, Durgā, by making use of the term *durgati*, meaning "distress."

avedyasaṃvedyapadam apadaṃ paramārthaḥ
padaṃ tu vedyasaṃvedyapadam eva hi yogināṃ

72. Stepping into licentiousness
is not stepping toward the highest goal.
For, indeed, only stepping into sanctioned behavior
is a step to be taken by *yogins*.

vedyaṃ saṃvedyate yasminn apāyādinibandhanam
tathāpravṛttibuddhyāpi stryādy āgamaviśuddhayā

73. In one who holds fast to knowing what is to be known,
such as the nature of destruction, and so on,
the intellect turns away from women, and so on,
in accordance with the purity of the scriptures.

tatpadaṃ sādhvavasthānād bhinnagranthyādilakṣanam
anvarthayogatas tantre vedyasaṃvedyam ucyate

74. That stage [that arises] from being situated in goodness,
marked by different text holders,
conforming to meaning derived from Yoga in the *tantra*,
is called "knowing what is to be known."

avedyasaṃvedyapadaṃ viparītam ato matam
bhavābhinandiviṣayaṃ samāropasamākulam

75. Stepping into licentiousness
is considered the opposite.
The one who rejoices in worldly existence
is greatly agitated by involvement with objects.

kṣudro lābharatir dīno matsarī bhayavān śaṭhaḥ
ajño bhavābhinandī syān niṣphalārambhasaṇgataḥ

76. The lover of worldly existence is vile,
finding pleasure in acquiring things,
wretched, wicked, filled with fear,
deceitful, engaged in undertakings that bear no fruit.

ity asatpariṇāmānuviddho bodho na sundaraḥ
tatsaṅgād eva niyamād viṣasampṛktakānnavat

77. Being full of negative transformations,
such an attitude is not pretty.
Even associating with it is invariably
like mixing food with poison.

etadvanto'ta eveha viparyāsaparā narāḥ
hitāhitavivekāndhāḥ khidyante sāmprateksiṇaḥ

78. Indeed, because of that,
such deluded persons are blind
when it comes to discriminating between right and wrong.
Their ability to see correctly is suppressed.

janmamṛtyujarāvyādhirogaśokādyupadrutam
vīkṣamāṇā api bhavaṃ nodvijante'timohataḥ

79. Despite seeing existence as oppressed by birth, death,
old age, disease, infirmity, sorrow, and so forth,
nonetheless, because of delusion,
they do not shrink from it.

kukṛtyaṃ kṛtyam ābhāti kṛtyaṃ cākrtyavat sadā
duḥkhe sukhadhiyākṛṣṭāḥ kacchūkaṇḍūyakādivat

80. They always see evil deeds as something to be done,
and do things that ought not be done.
They see pleasure in suffering,
as if drawn to scratch a scab.

yathā kaṇḍūyaneṣv eṣāṃ dhīr na kacchūnivartate
bhogāṅgeṣu tathaiteṣāṃ na tadicchāparikṣaye

81. Just as in such itching
there is no thought of the impact on the scabs,
so for those ensconsed in enjoyment
there is no abating of desire.

ātmānaṃ pāśayanty ete sadā'saccesṭayā bhṛśam
pāpadhūlyā jaḍāḥ kāryam avicāryaiva tattvataḥ

82. They bind themselves,
violent with desire,
always in darkness,
rendered stupid by the dust of their sin,
never considering truth.

dharmabījaṃ paraṃ prāpya mānuṣyaṃ karmabhūmiṣu
na satkarmakṛṣāv asya prayatante'lpamedhasaḥ

83. Having obtained the highest seed of *dharmas*
among the human realms of karma,
they do not strive with even a little sacrifice
on this earth for true action.

baḍiśāmiṣavat tucche kusukhe dāruṇodaye
saktās tyajanti sacceṣṭāṃ dhig aho dāruṇaṃ tamaḥ

84. Like baited meat on a fishhook they are addicted
to vanity, decadent pleasures, and cruel behavior.
Cruel and lethargic, they renounce the true object of desire.
What a pity!

avedyasaṃvedyapadam āndhyaṃ durgatipātakṛt
satsaṅgāgamayogena jeyam etan mahātmabhiḥ

85. Stepping into licentiousness
is the blindness that makes one fall into unhappiness.
This is to be overcome by great souls
through the Yoga of good company and sacred doctrine.

A CRITIQUE OF FALLACIOUS ARGUMENT (KUTARKA) (VERSES 86–97)

jīyamāne ca niyamād etasmiṃs tattvato nṛṇām
nivartate svato'tyantaṃ kutarkaviṣamagrahaḥ

86. Recognizing the incongruity of fallacious argument
and how people are truly oppressed by it,
one turns away from it entirely of one's own accord
by means of the observances.

bodharogaḥ śamāpayaḥ śraddhābhaṅgo'bhimānakṛt
kutarkaś cetaso vyktaṃ bhāvaśatrur anekadhā

87. Fallacious argument produces in the mind
sickness of intellect, destruction of equanimity,
disturbance of faith and cultivation of pride.
In many ways, it is the enemy of existence.

kutarke'bhiniveśas tan na yukto muktivādinām
yuktaḥ punaḥ śrute śīle samādhau ca mahātmanām

88. The proponents of liberation
are not tied to the pursuit of these fallacious arguments.
However, the great souled ones are joined
to scripture, good action, and *samādhi.*

bījaṃ cāsya paraṃ siddham avandhyaṃ sarvayoginām
parārthakaraṇaṃ yena pariśuddham ato'tra ca

89. The seed of this is the unbounded,
higher power of all *yogins*.
Through it, higher purpose is crafted.
Purity comes from this here, indeed.

avidyāsaṅgatāḥ prāyo vikalpāḥ sarva eva yat
tadyojanātmakaś caiṣa kutarkaḥ kim anena tat

90. Just as all suppositions (*vikalpa*s)
are largely associated with ignorance (*avidyā*),
so fallacious argument (*kutarka*) has for itself such a bond.
How can that be free from fault?

jātiprāyaś ca sarvo'yaṃ pratītiphalabādhitaḥ
hastī vyāpādayatyuktau prāptāprāptavikalpavat

91. This destroys existence and everything,
and is incompatible with the evidence of faith.
It is said that "an elephant is killed."
It is like imagining that this either has happened or has not happened.

This might be an allusion to Yudhiṣṭhira's famous lie in the *Mahābhārata*.

svabhāvottaraparyanta eṣo'sāv api tattvataḥ
nārvāgdṛggocaro nyāyād anyathā'nyena kalpitaḥ

92. "This indeed here is the truth,
the essence of the outer edge."
The field is not seen when approached by faulty logic.
It is accomplished in some other way.

ato'gniḥ kledayaty ambusannidhau dahatīti ca
ambv agnisannidhau tatsvābhāvyād ity udite tayoḥ

93. "With respect to the nature of the proximity of water and fire:
when near, fire wets and
when near, water burns."
In saying this about the two,

kośapānād ṛte jñānopāyo nāsty atra yuktitaḥ
viprakṛṣṭo'py ayaskāntaḥ svārthakṛd dṛśyate yataḥ

94. ... no method of knowledge is engaged here
—as in the norm that comes from imbibing from the storeroom [of wisdom].
Thus based on one's own interests, one will see what one wishes,
even if far removed [from the truth].

dṛṣṭāntamātraṃ sarvatra yad evaṃ sulabhaṃ kṣitau
etatpradhānas tat kena svanītyāpodyate hy ayam

95. This is only ever an analogy;
what is easy to grasp gets worn out.
Who brings about the origin of things?
This indeed is moistened by one's own moral behavior.

dvicandrasvapnavijñānanidarśanabalotthitaḥ
nirālambanatāṃ sarvajñānānāṃ sādhayan yathā

96. Making something firm
out of all knowledges which lack support
is like [assuming] that strong evidence is produced
by the perception of two moons in a dream.

sarvaṃ sarvatra cāpnoti yad asmād asamañjasam
pratītibādhitaṃ loke tad anena na kiñcana

97. "Everything everywhere is obtained."
That which comes from this is unbecoming (does not conform to reality).
This is not compatible with what is evident in the world.
By this, there is not anything at all.

THE IMPORTANCE OF ACTION, SCRIPTURE, AND FAITH (VERSES 98–101)

atīndriyārthasiddhyartham yathālocitakāriṇām
prayāsaḥ śuṣkatarkasya na cāsau gocaraḥ kvacit

98. For the sake of going beyond the senses,
and for the sake of power, thus actions are considered.
Exertion at barren cogitation
yields nothing whatsoever in this field.

gocaras tv āgamasyaiva tatas tadupalabdhitaḥ
candrasūryoparāgādisaṃvādyāgamadaraśanāt

99. But the field of the scriptures
[allows for] the understanding of this.
After viewing the scriptures, one comes into alignment,
as in the eclipse of the sun by the moon.

etatpradhānaḥ sacchrāddhaḥ śīlavān yogatatparaḥ
jānāty atīndriyān arthāṃs tathā cāha mahāmatiḥ

100. The origin of this is true faith.
The one possessing morality [attains] that highest Yoga.
Thus it is true that the great-minded
one knows goals beyond the senses.

āgamenānumānena yogābhyāsarasena ca
tridhā prakalpayan prajñāṃ labhate tattvam uttamam

101. Through scripture, inferences,
and the essence of Yoga practice,
they succeed at threefold wisdom
and obtain the highest reality (*tattva*).

THE ONENESS OF OMNISCIENCE (VERSES 102–109)

na tattvato bhinnamatāḥ sarvajñā bahavo yataḥ
mohas tadadhimuktīnāṃ tadbhedāśrayaṇaṃ tataḥ

102. Since the many omniscient ones
do not have divided thoughts regarding reality,

it is thus a delusion to be inclined to regard
that it has many distinctions.

sarvajño nāma yaḥ kaścit pāramārthika eva hi
sa eka eva sarvatra vyaktibhede'pi tattvataḥ

103. Anyone who is called omniscient
has obtained the highest purpose indeed.
He is essentially one everywhere,
though there may be differences in individuality.

pratipattis tatas tasya sāmānyenaiva yāvatām
te sarve'pi tam āpannā iti nyāyamatiḥ parā

104. Logicians would conclude that
inasmuch as they have attained omniscience,
they all have something
in common.

viśeṣas tu punas tasya kārtsnyenāsarvadarśibhiḥ
sarvair na jñāyate tena tam āpanno na kaścana

105. On the other hand, the distinction
with respect to one [who has acquired omniscience]
is that nothing in particular is unknown
by all of those who have the right understanding.

tasmāt sāmānyato'py enam abhyupaiti ya eva hi
nirvyājaṃ tulya evāsau tenāṃśenaiva dhīmatām

106. Indeed, they say,
"Thus in entering into this state [of omniscience] there is a commonality."
For a wise one, the undisputed [nature of Omniscience]
is always the same.

yathaivaikaṣya nṛpater bahavo'pi samāśritāḥ
dūrāsannādibhede'pi tadbhṛtyāḥ sarva eva te

107. Just as one king has many dependents,
divided according to whether they are near or far, and so on,
nonetheless, all of them are indeed servants.

sarvajñatattvābhedena tathā sarvajñavādinaḥ
sarve tattattvagā jñeyā bhinnācārasthitā api

108. So also there is no distinction
in the essence of omniscience.
The definition of omniscience is that all principles are known,
and one's comportment and discernment are stable.

na bheda eva tattvena sarvajñānāṃ mahātmanām
tathā nāmādibhede'pi bhāvyam etan mahātmabhiḥ

109. In essence, there is no distinction
between the great souls who have omniscience,
despite distinctions of name, and so on.
This is to be perceived by the great souls.

DEVOTION TO ONE OR MANY GODS (VERSES 110–114)

citrācitravibhāgena yac ca deveṣu varṇitā
bhaktiḥ sadyogaśātreṣu tato'py evam idaṃ sthitam

110. Devotion can be directed to either one god or many gods.
Just as the devotion itself remains the same regardless,
so also omniscience is single,
regardless of who or how many have obtained it.

saṃsāriṣu hi deveṣu bhaktis tatkāyagāminām
tadatīte punas tattve tadatītārthāyinām

111. Devotion to the worldly deities
is pursued by those in the body.
In essence, they are gone again,
gone with the purpose of travelling on [and being reborn].

citrā cādyeṣu tadrāgatadanyadveṣasaṅgatā
acitrā carame tv eṣā śamasārā'khilaiva hi

112. In variegated [worship], one's days are linked
with desire and repulsion.
In the focused [worship], devoted to one [ideal],
there is tranquility, power, and a sense of totality.

saṃsāraiṇāṃ hi devānāṃ yasmāc citrāṇy anekadhā
sthityaiśvaryaprabhāvādyaiḥ sthānāni pratiśāsanam

113. Since there are variations of numerous sorts
among the deities of this mundane existence,
they are placed in their ranks
according to their duration, power, eminence, and so forth.

tasmāt tatsādhanopāyo niyamāc citra eva hi
na bhinnanagarāṇaṃ syād ekaṃ vartma kadācana

114. Therefore, based on observances,
the disciplines and practices
[exhibit] distinct differences.
There could never be a single road to different cities.

THE NATURE OF SACRIFICIAL ACTION (VERSES 115–118)

iṣṭāpūrtāni karmāṇi loke citrābhisandhitaḥ
nānāphalāni sarvāṇi dṛṣṭavyāni vicakṣaṇaiḥ

115. That all pious works and worldly actions
bring about different fruits
appropriate to the various motivations
is to be seen through one's own eyes.

ṛtvigbhir mantrasaṃskārair brāhmaṇānāṃ samakṣataḥ
antarvedyāṃ hi yad dattaṃ iṣṭaṃ tad abhidhīyate

116. For sacrifice is defined as that which is given
within the sacred ground in the presence of brahmins,
along with ceremonial *mantras*
and sacrifices offered at the right time.

vāpīkūpataḍāgāni devatāyatanāni ca
annapradānam etat tu pūrtaṃ tattvavido viduḥ

117. But the wise know that this is
the true essence of pious works:

construction of wells, ponds, and tanks,
and sanctuaries for the gods and the offering of food.

This verse seems to speak from a sensitivity to issues of "social justice," as there is a suggestion that public works that benefit the social community are in some sense more meritorious than solely making symbolic offerings in pious rituals, as discussed in the preceding verse.

abhisandheḥ phalaṃ bhinnam anuṣṭhāne same'pi hi
paramo'taḥ sa eveha vārīva kṛṣikarmaṇi

118. In the same religious practice,
it is the intention that causes a different fruit;
this [intention] is of greatest importance,
like water to agriculture.

THE CENTRALITY OF INDIVIDUALITY (VERSE 119)

rāgādibhir ayaṃ ceha bhidyate'nekadhā nṛṇām
nānāphalopabhoktṝṇāṃ tathā buddhyādibhedataḥ

119. People differ in various ways
due to their desires, and so forth.
They enjoy various fruits according to differences
in their intellectual dispositions, and so on.

INTELLECT, KNOWLEDGE, AND NON-DELUDEDNESS (VERSES 120–128)

buddhir jñānam asammohas trividho bodha iṣyate
tadbhedāt sarvakarmāṇi bhidyante sarvadehinām

120. A threefold awakening is proclaimed:
intellect, knowledge, and non-deludedness.
All actions of all beings are to be distinguished
on the basis of that distinction.

Note that the triplicity of *buddhi*, *jñāna*, and *asammoha* (intellect, knowledge, and non-deludedness) stands in contrasting position to the tantric triplicity of *icchā*, *śakti*, and *kriyā* (desire, power, and action).

indriyārthāśrayā buddhir jñānam tv āgamapūrvakam
sadanuṣṭhānavac caitad asammoho'bhidhīyate

121. Intellect (*buddhi*) is the support for the objects of the senses,
while knowledge (*jñāna*) is derived from the ancient scripture.
Herein, non-deludedness (*asammoha*) is described
as "true religious practice."

ratnopalambhatajjñānatatprāptyādi yathākraman
ihodāharaṇaṃ sādhu jñeyaṃ buddhyādisiddhaye

122. Knowledge is like perceiving a jewel;
the next step is obtaining it.
Saying it is good, the intellect realizes
it is to be known in order to obtain success.

ādaraḥ karaṇe prītir avighnaḥ sampadāgamaḥ
jijñāsā tajjñasevā ca sadanuṣṭhānalakṣaṇam

123. The mark of true religious practice
is joy in exerting oneself, an absence of obstacles,
proficiency in scripture, desire to know,
and homage to the knowledgeable.

buddhipūrvāṇi karmāṇi sarvāṇy eveha dehinām
saṃsāraphaladāny eva vipākavirasatvataḥ

124. All actions performed by a living creature
based on prior understanding
certainly yield the fruits of *saṃsāra*,
owing to the unpleasantness of the ripening.

jñānapūrvāṇi tāny eva muktyaṅgaṃ kulayoginām
śrutaśaktisamāveśād anubandhaphalatvataḥ

125. By the Kula Yogis,
these are considered as adjuncts to liberation.
This can be seen from their combination
  of texts and [teachings on] power,
and from the fruits of their attachment.

asaṃmohasamutthāni tv ekāntapariśuddhitaḥ
nirvāṇaphaladāny āśu bhavātītārthayāyinām

126. But the taking up of non-deludedness leads to singular purity;
it gives the fruit of *nirvāṇa* quickly
to those traveling with the purpose
of going beyond worldly existence.

prākṛteṣv iha bhāveṣu yeṣāṃ ceto nirutsukam
bhavabhogaviraktās te bhavātītārthayāyinaḥ

127. Those who are indifferent to manifestations of worldly existence
and hold no interest in enjoying worldly existence
travel with the purpose
of going beyond worldly existence.

eka eva tu mārgo'pi teṣāṃ śamaparāyaṇaḥ
avasthābhedabhede'pi jaladhau tīramārgavat

128. For those whose goal is calmness,
there is indeed only one path.
On this distinct [path] there abides no distinction
like the path on the shore of a lake.

THE NATURE OF NIRVĀṆA (VERSES 129–133)

saṃsārātītatattvaṃ tu paraṃ nirvāṇasaṃjñitaṃ
taddhy ekam eva niyamāc chabdabhede'pi tattvataḥ

129. The highest essence of going beyond *saṃsāra*
is called "*nirvāṇa*." The wisdom gained from discipline
is singular in essence,
though heard of in different ways.

sadāśivaḥ paraṃbrahma siddhātmā tathateti ca
śabdais tad ucyate'nvarthād ekam evaivamādibhiḥ

130. "Eternal Śiva, Highest Brahman, Accomplished Soul, Suchness":
With these words one refers to it,
though the meaning is one
in all the various forms.

tallakṣaṇāvisaṃvādān nirābādham anāmayam
niṣkriyaṃ ca paraṃ tattvaṃ yato janmādyayogataḥ

131. The mark of that highest essence (teaching) is,
with no contradiction,
free from disturbance, disease, and action,
by which one is freed from birth, and so on.

jñāte nirvāṇatattve'sminn asaṃmohena tattvataḥ
prekṣāvatāṃ na tadbhaktau vivāda upapadyate

132. Through calmness and from the principles,
one is established in knowledge of the essence of *nirvāṇa*.
Among the considerate, there is no dispute
regarding devotion to this [*nirvāṇa*].

sarvajñapūrvakaṃ caitan niyamād eva yatsthitam
āsanno'yam ṛjur mārgas tadbhedas tat kathaṃ bhavet

133. The one who has been situated in omniscience
has done so due to discipline.
The ones near to this [have found] the straight path.
How could there be any distinction?

THE NEED TO RESPECT MULTIPLE TEACHINGS
(VERSES 134–152)

citrā tu deśanaiteṣāṃ syād vineyānuguṇyataḥ
yasmād ete mahātmāno bhavavyādhibhiṣagvarāḥ

134. The variety of teaching is suited
according to who is being taught.
These great souls are the best healers
of the sickness known as "worldly existence."

yasya yena prakāreṇa bījādhānādisaṃbhavaḥ
sānubandho bhavaty ete tathā tasya jagus tataḥ

135. Just as it may be said that grain, and so forth,
is born from the seed in a particular way,
so it may be said of the movement of [omniscient ones].

ekāpi deśanaiteṣāṃ yadvā śrotṛvibhedataḥ
acintyapuṇyasāmarthyāt tathā citrā'vabhāsate

136. Perhaps the teaching is one
but there are various people who hear it.
On account of the inconceivable merit it bestows,
it shines forth in various ways.

yathābhavyaṃ ca sarveṣām upakāro'pi tatkṛtaḥ
jāyate'vandhyatā'py evam asyāḥ sarvatra susthitā

137. This auspicious [teaching]
provides benefit for everyone.
Indeed, the essence of freedom
is born joyously of it at all times.

yadvā tattannayāpekṣā tattatkālādiyogataḥ
ṛṣibhyo deśanā citrā tanmūlaiṣāpi tattvataḥ

138. The root of the variety of teaching taught by the seers,
though stemming from essentials,
can be attributed to various perspectives
on conduct or from time, and so forth.

tadabhiprāyam ajñātvā na tato'rvāgdṛśāṃ satām
yujyate tatpratikṣepo mahānarthakaraḥ paraḥ

139. Not having known the intention,
it is not possible to assess the status;
there would be no purpose in forumlating objections
regarding [the thought of] the great one who has gone
beyond.

niśānāthapratikṣepo yathā'ndhānām asaṅgataḥ
tadbhedaparikalpaś ca tathaivārvāgdṛśām ayam

140. Just as the blind are not inclined
to dispute with one who possesses sight,
so also the settling of such distinctions
is not to be made from a lower point of view.

na yujyate pratikṣepaḥ sāmānyasyāpi tatsatām
āryāpavādas tu punar jihvāchedādhiko mataḥ

141. Hence it is not proper
to object to words of reconciliation.
Refuting or reviling noble people, it seems,
would be worse than cutting one's own tongue.

kudṛṣṭyādivan no santo bhāṣante prāyaśaḥ kvacit
niścitaṃ sāravac caiva kintu sattvārthakṛt sadā

142. Saintly persons never speak
like evil-minded people.
They speak definitively and meaningfully,
but always acting with good intention.

niścayo'tīndriyārthasya yogijñānād ṛte ca na
ato'py atrāndhakalpānāṃ vivādena na kiñcana

143. There can be no certainty with regard to objects
beyond the senses without *yogic* knowledge,
therefore, there is nothing [to be gained] here
through a contest of blind alternatives.

na cānumānaviṣaya eṣo'rthas tattvato mataḥ
na cāto niścayaḥ samyag anyatrāpy āha dhīdhanaḥ

144. These essential matters are not objects
that can be inferred with the mind
and, moreover, there is no distinct certainty otherwise.
Thus it has been said by one gifted with wisdom.

yatnenānumito'py arthaḥ kuśalair anumātṛbhiḥ
abhiyuktatarair anyair anyathaivopapādyate

145. With effort, even a position inferred
through the proper establishment of premises
may certainly be approached in another way,
being assailed by opponents.

jñāyeran hetuvādena padārthā yady atīndriyāḥ
kālenaitāvatā prājñaiḥ kṛtaḥ syāt teṣu niścayaḥ

146. If the meaning of those things beyond the senses
could be known through a statement of reason,
then by now it would have been ascertained by the scholars.

na caitad evaṃ yat tasmāc chuṣkatarkagraho mahān
mithyābhimānahetutvāt tyājya eva mumukṣubhiḥ

147. But since this is not the case,
then those great graspers at unprofitable argument
due to pride and ignorance
should be renounced by those desirous of liberation.

grahaḥ sarvatra tattvena mumukṣūṇām asaṅgataḥ
muktau dharmā api prāyas tyaktavyāḥ kim anena tat

148. In reality, those desirous of liberation
should have no attachment to grasping anywhere.
In liberation, even *dharmas*, for the most part, are to be renounced.
Why not this?

tadatra mahatāṃ vartma samāśritya vicakṣaṇaiḥ
vartitavyaṃ yathānyāyaṃ tadatikramavarjitaiḥ

149. Thus the path of the great ones
is to be depended upon by the clear-sighted ones.
Such logic is to be carried out (observed)
by those avoiding transgressions.

parapīḍeha sūkṣmāpi varjanīyā prayatnataḥ
tadvat tadupakāre'pi yatitavyaṃ sadaiva hi

150. Even the slightest of pain to others
is to be avoided with great effort.
Along with this
one should strive to be helpful at all times.

guravo devatā viprā yatayaś ca tapodhanāḥ
pūjanīyā mahātmānaḥ suprayatnena cetasā

151. Teachers, gods, the learned,
the renouncers, and the doers of austerities:
these great souls should be revered
with a mind well applied.

pāpavatsv api cātyantaṃ svakarmanihateṣv alam
anukampaiva sattveṣu nyāyyā dharmo'yam uttamaḥ

152. Even in regard to those with excessive sin
who have been cut down by their own actions,
one should have compassion for those beings,
according to the logic of this highest *dharma*.

STHIRĀ (FIRM) YOGA (VERSES 153–161)

kṛtam atra prasaṅgena prakṛtaṃ prastumo'dhunā
tatpunaḥ pañcamī tāvad yogadṛṣṭir mahodayā

153. We are finished now with our digression.
Now we will resume what was under discussion.
We return to the fifth,
the Yoga view that leads to liberation.

sthirāyāṃ darśanaṃ nityaṃ pratyāhāravad eva ca
kṛtyam abhrāntam anaghaṃ sūkṣmabodhasamanvitam

154. In the Sthirā (Firm) view,
one is always as if in a state of sensory withdrawal [Patañjali].
One's actions are faultless and unmuddied [Bhadanta Bhāskara],
and one is endowed with subtle awakening [Bandhu Bhagavaddatta].

bāladhūlīgṛhakrīḍātulyā'syāṃ bhāti dhīmatām
tamogranthivibhedena bhavaceṣṭākhilaiva hi

155. Through the undoing of the knot of lethargy,
the entire struggle of worldly existence
is perceived by the wise as like children
playing with a house made of sand.

māyā marīci gandharva nagara svapna sannibhān
bāhyān paśyati tattvena bhāvān śruta vivekataḥ

156. From discrimination gleaned from scripture, and with truth,
one sees all external existence
as if it resembles a dream,
the city of the Gandharvas,
a magician's illusion.

abāhyaṃ kevalaṃ jyotir nirābādham anāmayam
yad atra tat paraṃ tattvaṃ śeṣaḥ punar upaplavaḥ

157. Here the only thing resembling truth
is the interior, singular, undisturbed, unnameable light.
Anything else is merely a disturbance.

evaṃ vivekino dhīrāḥ pratyāhāraparās tathā
dharmabādhāparityāgayatnavantaś ca tattvataḥ

158. Thus those who are firm in their discrimination
excel at detatchment,
renouncing obstacles to *dharma*
and exerting genuine effort.

na hy alakṣamīsakhī lakṣmīr yathānandāya dhīmatām
tathā pāpasakhā loke dehināṃ bhogavistaraḥ

159. For the wise, wealth does not bring happiness,
because its friend is poverty.
So should it be for the many
extensive enjoyments of the body,
which in the world have sin as their companion.

dharmād api bhavan bhogaḥ prāyo'narthāya dehinām
candanād api saṃbhūto dahaty eva hutāśanaḥ

160. Even enjoyment arising from *dharma*
is worthless for the path of a living being.
Even if it is arising from the best of woods (sandalwood),
it burns and is consumed by fire.

bhogāt tadicchāviratiḥ skandhabhārāpanuttaye
skandhāntarasamāropas tatsaṃskāravidhānataḥ

161. Trying to stop desire through enjoyment
is like removing a burden from one shoulder
and placing it on the other shoulder.
Like that, karmic residue (*saṃskāra*) is created.

KĀNTĀ (PLEASING) YOGA (VERSES 162–169)

kāntāyām etad anyeṣāṃ prītaye dhāraṇā parā
ato'tra nānyam unnityaṃ mīmāṃsā'sti hitodayā

162. In Kāntā (Pleasing), there is a higher concentration
[Patañjali] for the sake of compassion toward others.
Pleasure is never found in externals [Bhadanta Bhāskara],
and a beneficial reflection arises [Bandhu Bhagavaddatta].

asyāṃ tu dharmamāhātmyāt samācāraviśuddhitaḥ
priyo bhavati bhūtānāṃ dharmaikāgramanās tathā

163. In this state, due to the efficacy of *dharma*,
one's conduct becomes purified.
One is beloved among beings
and single-mindedly devoted to *dharma*.

śrutadharme mano nityaṃ kāyas tvasyānyaceṣṭite
atas tv ākṣepakajñānān na bhogā bhavahetavaḥ

164. With mind always fixed on scriptural *dharma*,
it is only the body that is busy with other things.
Thus renouncing due to knowledge,
enjoyments are not causes for a return to worldly existence.

māyāmbhas tattvataḥ paśyann anudvignastato drutam
tanmadhyena prayāty eva yathā vyāghātavarjitaḥ

165. Just as in seeing the truth behind the illusion of water
one's mind is put at ease
and one can go forth quickly through,
so it is with avoiding obstacles.

bhogān svarūpataḥ paśyaṃs tathā māyodakopamān
bhuñjāno'pi hy asaṅgaḥ san prayāty eva paraṃ padam

166. Seeing the true form of enjoyment
is like the illusion of water.
Being detached even while enjoying,
one goes forth to the highest step.

bhogatattvasya tu punar na bhavodadhilaṅghanam
māyodakadṛḍhāveśas tena yātīha kaḥ pathā

167. Again, one for whom enjoyments are real
never crosses over the ocean of existence.
After firmly immersing oneself in the waters of illusion,
how is one able to go on the path?

sa tatraiva bhavodvigno yathā tiṣṭhaty asaṃśayam
mokṣamārge'pi hi tathā bhogajambālamohitaḥ

168. Even when distressed with worldly existence,
such a person stays there without doubt.
Thus it is in regard to the path of liberation
for the one deluded by the strength of what is born of enjoyment.

mīmāṃsābhāvato nityaṃ na moho'syāṃ yato bhavet
atas tattvasamāveśāt sadaiva hi hitodayaḥ

169. Here there is always reflection on the nature of existence,
and hence there could be no delusion.
Thus there is a commitment to (penetration into) truth,
and benefits always arise.

PRABHĀ (RADIANT) YOGA (VERSES 170–177)

dhyānapriyā prabhā prāyo nāsyāṃ rug ata eva hi
tattvapratipattiyutā viśeṣeṇa śamānvitā

170. In Prabhā (Radiant),
one frequently practices meditation [Patañjali] that is pleasing.
In this there is no suffering [Bhadanta Bhāskara].

It is accompanied by knowledge of the truth [Bandhu Bhagavaddatta]
and a remarkable calmness.

dhyānajaṃ sukham asyāṃ tu jitamanmathasādhanam
vivekabalanirjātaṃ śamasāraṃ sadaiva hi

171. In this, happiness is born of meditation,
as well as the discipline of conquering amorous passion,
the emergence of strong discrimination,
and the power of constant serenity.

sarvaṃ paravaśaṃ duḥkhaṃ sarvam ātmavaśaṃ sukham
etad uktaṃ samāsena lakṣaṇaṃ sukhaduḥkhayoḥ

172. "All suffering [is dependent on] externals;
all happiness [is dependent on] oneself."
This saying, in brief,
gives the characteristics of pleasure and pain.

puṇyāpekṣam api hy evam sukhaṃ paravaśaṃ sthitam
tataś ca duḥkham evaitat tallakṣaṇaniyogataḥ

173. Even what appears to be merit in fact
is situated in external happiness.
Hence, it is actually pain,
in accordance with this characteristic.

dhyānaṃ ca nirmale bodhe sadaiva hi mahātmanām
kṣīṇaprāyamalaṃ hema sadā kalyāṇam eva hi

174. Due to their intellect being purified,
the great souls meditate.
Gold with diminished impurity
is always pretty indeed.

satpravṛttipadaṃ cehāsaṅgānuṣṭhānasaṅgatam
mahāpathaprayāṇaṃ yad anāgāmipadāvaham

175. This truly perfect stage allows one
to stand unattached in the midst of attachment.

The one who follows this great path
arrives at the stage of not returning.

praśāntavāhitāsaṃjñaṃ visabhāgaparikṣayaḥ
śivavartma dhruvādhveti yogibhir gīyate hy adaḥ

176. By the *yogins* this is called peace bearing and
having no share in destruction,
[it is the] auspicious path,
and the constant course.

etat prasādhayaty āśu yad yogy asyāṃ vyavasthitaḥ
etat padāvahaiṣaiva tat tatraitadvidāṃ matā

177. This brings success quickly
for the *yogin* established in this.
This indeed produces the stage there.
This is the thought of the wise.

PARĀ (HIGHEST) YOGA (VERSES 178–186)

samādhiniṣṭhā tu parā tadāsaṅgavivarjitā
sātmīkṛtapravṛttiś ca taduttīrṇāśayeti ca

178. But the Parā (Highest) is *samādhi* [Patañjali].
It frees one from attachment [Bhadanta Bhāskara].
One manifests all actions as not different from that of the Self
[Bandhu Bhagavaddatta]. One resides in a state of liberation.

nirācārapado hy asyām aticāravivarjitaḥ
ārūḍhārohaṇābhāvagativat tv asya ceṣṭitam

179. The behavior of such a one
is like the manner of one who,
having climbed up [a mountain],
no longer is in the state of climbing.

ratnādiśikṣādṛgbhyo'nyā yathā dṛk tanniyojane
tathācārakriyā'py asya saivānyā phalabhedataḥ

180. Just as one who is trained in looking at jewels and so forth
is different from the one who is merely enjoined to look at
them,

so the action and conduct of such a one are different
due to the distinction of the fruit it bears.

tanniyogān mahātmeha kṛtakṛtyo yathā bhavet
tathā'yaṃ dharmasaṃnyāsaviniyogān mahāmuniḥ

181. Just as the order followed by the great soul
who has done what is to be done (would be unique),
so it is for this great sage,
due to the order established by the renunciation of *dharma*.

dvitīyāpūrvakaraṇe mukhyo'yam upajāyate
kevalaśrīs tataś cāsya niḥsapatnā sadodayā

182. This culmination is born
of the second *apūrvakaraṇa* (that is, the Elimination Ladder).
This has the radiance of *kevala* (perfect knowledge).
Freedom from all adversity arises.

sthitaḥ śitāṃśuvaj jīvaḥ prakṛtyā bhāvaśuddhayā
candrikāvac ca vijñānaṃ tadāvaraṇam abhravat

183. With the various species of karma in a purified state,
the *jīva* becomes established in cool, moonlike radiance.
With respect to this, ordinary consciousness
is like a cloud concealing the moonlight.

ghātikarmābhrakalpaṃ taduktayogānilāhateḥ
yadā'paiti tadā śrīmān jāyate jñānakevalī

184. It is said that at the time
when the clouds of destructive karma
are themselves destroyed by the wind of Yoga,
that is the escape.
Then the glory of singular knowledge is born.

kṣīṇadoṣo'tha sarvajñaḥ sarvalabdhiphalānvitaḥ
paraṃ parārthaṃ saṃpādya toto yogāntam aśnute

185. With faults eliminated, omniscient,
endowed with the fruits of all that can be accomplished,
with things to be done now only for the sake of others,
such a one attains the end of Yoga.

tatra drāg eva bhagavān ayogād yogasattamāt
bhavavyādhikṣayaṃ kṛtvā nirvāṇaṃ labhate param

186. Therein the blessed one quickly attains highest *nirvāṇa*
through the Yoga of Total Freedom,
the best of Yogas,
having accomplished the cessation
of the ailment of worldly existence.

THE NATURE OF LIVING LIBERATION (VERSES 187–192)

vyādhimuktaḥ pumān loke yādṛśas tādṛśo hy ayam
nābhāvo na ca no mukto vyādhināvyādhito na ca

187. A person liberated from an ailment is still in the world.
Like that, so is this [liberated person].
It is not that he is nonexistent;
it is not that he is not liberated;
nor that he had not been afflicted with an ailment.

bhava eva mahāvyādhir janmamṛtyuvikāravān
vicitramohajananas tīvrarāgādivedanaḥ

188. Existence, indeed, is a great illness,
comprised of birth, death, and disease.
It produces various forms of delusion
and causes the sensation of excessive desire, and so forth.

mukhyo'yam ātmano'nādicitrakarmanidānajaḥ
tathānubhavasiddhatvāt sarvaprāṇabhṛtām iti

189. This is the chief (ailment) of the soul:
giving birth without beginning
to the cause of various karmas.
All living beings understand this experience.

etanmuktaś ca mukto'pi mukhya evopapadyate
janmādidoṣavigamāt tadadoṣatvasaṅgateḥ

190. When liberated from this,
one reaches the prime state of liberation.

From the cessation of the fault of birth, and so forth,
one encounters that state of faultlessness.

tatsvabhāvopamarde'pi tattatsvābhāvyayogataḥ
tasyaiva hi tathābhāvāt tadadoṣatvasaṅgatiḥ

191. In the cessation of that essence (of rebirth, etc.),
and from union with the nonexistence of that,
he has indeed been [freed] from worldly existence
and joined to the state of faultlessness.

svabhāvo'sya svabhāvo yan nijā sattaiva tattvataḥ
bhāvāvadhir ayaṃ yukto nānyathā'tiprasaṅgataḥ

192. The essence of this is essence,
meaning innate existence derived from its principle.
Being joined to this leads to the termination of worldly existence.
It is not otherwise due to an "unwarrantable stretch of a rule."

A CRITIQUE OF SARVĀSTIVĀDIN BUDDHISM
(VERSES 193–197)

anantarakṣaṇābhūtir ātmabhūteha yasya tu
tayā'virodhān nityo'sau syād asan vā sadaiva hi

193. The defender of endless nonexistence
would in fact defend the existence of the Self,
because, by this argument, there is no resistance to the notion of eternalness:
it would be either nonexistent or be always.

sa eva na bhavaty etad anyathābhavatītivat
viruddhaṃ tannayād eva tadutpattyāditas tathā

194. "This indeed does not exist [now];
this exists in a different manner."
This is contrary to reason,
as are arguments arising from this later.

sato'sattve tadutpādas tato nāśo'pi tasya yat
tannaṣṭasya punar bhāvaḥ sadā nāśe na tatsthitiḥ

195. If a thing arises from nonexistence,
then there will be the destruction of that thing.
The existence of it would be destroyed again.
Something that is always being destroyed cannot be posited.

sa kṣaṇasthitidharmā ced dvitīyādikṣaṇesthitau
yujyate hy etad apy asya tathā coktānatikramaḥ

196. That *dharma* (phenomenon) that exists for a moment
would then exist in the next moment;
the first would be joined by it.
Hence, what was said is not contradicted.

kṣaṇasthitau tadaivāsya nāsthitir yuktyasaṅgateḥ
na paścād api sety evaṃ sato'sattvaṃ vyavasthitam

197. Emphatic affirmation of duration
on the basis of two momentary durations is equivocation.
It simply does not follow.
The reality of being is not established by this [line of reasoning].

A CRITIQUE OF MONISM (VERSES 198–203)

bhavabhāvānivṛttāv apy uktā muktakalpanā
ekāntaikasvabhāvasya na hy avasthādvayaṃ kvacit

198. The conception of liberation is unworkable
unless there is assent to the notion of the cessation of worldly existence.
If only a singular essence is proclaimed,
then there could never be the two states of life (viz., happiness and misery).

tadabhāve ca saṃsārī muktaś ceti nirarthakam
tatsvabhāvopamardo'sya nītyā tāttvika iṣyatām

199. It would be senseless to say there is
no difference between the liberated one and one in bondage.

In this there is the destruction of that essence
[that binds one to *saṃsāra*] through one's conduct;
one should seek this as the truth.

didṛkṣādyātmabhūtaṃ tanmukhyam asyā nivartate
pradhānādinater hetus tadabhāvān na tannatiḥ

200. Desiring to see, and so forth, are elements of the self.
The first principle is that
this can be reversed.
The cause of this is the posturing of materiality.
When it is rendered nonexistent, there is no longer any posturing.

anyathā syād iyaṃ nityam eṣā ca bhava ucyate
evaṃ ca bhavanityatve kathaṃ muktasya sambhavaḥ

201. By some, this [materiality] is called eternal,
yet this is called "worldly existence."
Thus all worldly existence would be called "eternal."
How could there be the possibility of liberation?

The above sequence of verses criticizes the Sāṃkhya philosophical view that the manifest world (*prakṛti*) is eternal.

avasthā tattvato no cen nanu tatpratyayaḥ katham
bhrānto'yam kim aneneti mānam atra na vidyate

202. But [it could be said] that appearance is not truth.
But how is this proven?
One might say, "This is all confusion; by this, what is known?"
This notion is not correct.

yogijñānaṃ tu mānaṃ cet tadavasthāntaraṃ tu tat
tataḥ kiṃ bhrāntam etat syād anyathā siddhasādhyatā

203. If it is said that this notion comprises *yogic* knowledge,
then it must be pointed out that
this (*yogic* knowledge) is [from a] different state.
What if this (*yogic* knowledge) were mere confusion?
[It is obviously not.] Hence, our position prevails.

Jainism asserts that appearance is real.

THE DISTINCTION BETWEEN WORLDLY EXISTENCE AND LIBERATION (VERSES 204–206)

vyādhitas tadabhāvo vā tadanyo vā yathaiva hi
vyādhimukto na sannītyā kadācid upapadyate

204. If an ailment is nonexistent (as per the Vedāntins),
or is something else (as the Buddhists claim),
then, according to either precept,
[a person] is never liberated from ailment.

saṃsārī tadabhāvo vā tadanyo vā tathaiva hi
mukto'pi hanta no mukto mukhyavṛttyeti tadvidaḥ

205. If the one in *saṃsāra* is nonexistent
or is in fact something else,
then a liberated one is not liberated!
This is the prevailing thought of the wise.

kṣīṇavyādhir yathā loke vyādhimukta iti sthitaḥ
bhavarogy eva tu tathā muktas tantreṣu tatkṣayāt

206. Just as in the world one whose illness has disappeared
is determined to be cured,
so also the one who has the disease of worldly existence.
In the *tantras* he is called liberated due to the destruction [of that disease].

THE PURPOSE OF WRITING THIS TEXT (VERSE 207)

anekayogaśāstrebhyaḥ saṃkṣepeṇa samuddhṛtaḥ
dṛṣṭibhedena yogo'yam ātmānusmṛtaye paraḥ

207. For the sake of my own recollection,
this chief (architechtonic) Yoga,
with reference is distinct views,
has been compiled in this brief exposition
based on the texts of several Yoga schools.

THE FOURFOLD DIVISION OF YOGA PRACTITIONERS (VERSES 208–213)

kulādiyogabhedena caturdhā yogino yataḥ
ataḥ paropakāro'pi leśato na virudhyate

208. Since the distinction of *yogins* is fourfold,
including the Family Yogins, and so forth,
then this small contribution
will not hinder helping others.

kulapravṛttacakrā ye ta evāsyādhikāriṇaḥ
yogino na tu sarve'pi tathā 'siddhyādibhāvataḥ

209. Those known as Family and Engaged [Yogins]
are entitled [to know this]
due to their states of accomplishment, and so on.

ye yogināṃ kule jātās taddharmānugatāś ca ye
kulayogina ucyante gotravanto'pi nāpare

210. Those who are born into a family of *yogin*s
and who follow that *dharma*
are called Family Yogins
and not those different ones called the Clan Yogins.

sarvatrādveṣiṇaś caite gurudevadvijapriyāh
dayālavo vinītāś ca bodhavanto yatendriyāḥ

211. These display no ill will anywhere,
think fondly of *guru*s, gods, and the twice-born,
are compassionate and modest, and
possess wisdom and control of the senses.

pravṛttacakrās tu punar yamadvayasamāśrayāḥ
śeṣadvayārthino'tyantaṃ śuśrūṣādiguṇānvitāḥ

212. And again the Engaged [Yogins] have taken recourse to two disciplines,
perpetually aspire to the remaining two,

and are endowed with the quality
of wanting to hear more [about scriptural matters].

ādyāvañcakayogāptyā tadanyadvayalābhinaḥ
ete'dhikāriṇo yogaprayogasyeti tadvidaḥ

213. Having obtained this Yoga of Primal Authenticity,
the other two are obtained.
These, then, are entitled to undertake Yoga,
according to those who know.

THE FOUR DISCIPLINES (YAMA) (VERSES 214–221)

ihāhiṃsādayaḥ pañca suprasiddhā yamāḥ satām
aparigrahaparyantās tathecchādicaturvidhāḥ

214. The five disciplines ranging from nonviolence
to nonpossession are well known,
as well as a fourfold division,
beginning with the Wishful (*icchā*).

tadvatkathāprītiyutā tathā'vipariṇāminī
yameṣvicchā'vaseyeha prathamo yama eva tu

215. Of these [four] disciplines,
the Wishful is to be clearly understood as the first discipline
and is characterized by a love of discussion that does
not change.

sarvatra śamasāraṃ tu yamapālanam eva yat
pravṛttir iha vijñeyā dvitīyo yama eva tat

216. The second discipline
is to be understood as Engaged,
the essence of which is ubiquitous calm
and a nourishing of the disciplines.

vipakṣacintārahitaṃ yamapālanam eva yat
tat sthairyam iha vijñeyaṃ tṛtīyo yama eva hi

217. The third discipline
is to be known as Firmness,

which also nourishes the disciplines,
and which makes one free from worry about the other side (i.e., worldly things).

parāthasādhakaṃ tv etat siddhiḥ śuddhāntarātmanaḥ
acintyaśaktiyogena caturtho yama eva tu

218. The fourth discipline
is accomplished by the Yoga of Inconceivable Power,
resulting in the perfection of unsurpassed purity of self
and goodness for the sake of others.

sadbhiḥ kalyāṇasampannair darśanād api pāvanaiḥ
tathādarśanato yoga ādyāvañcaka ucyate

219. From being with the auspicious adepts
and from *darśana* with a purified one,
there arises the vision
called the "Yoga of Primal Authenticity."

teṣām eva praṇāmādikriyāniyama ity alam
kriyāvañcakayogaḥ syān mahāpāpakṣayodayaḥ

220. Observance includes such actions
as bowing, and so forth, to those [great beings].
The action of Authentic Yoga would result
in the arising of the diminishment of great sin.

phalāvañcakayogas tu sadbhya eva niyogataḥ
sānubandhaphalāvāptir dharmasiddhau satāṃ matā

221. But the fruit of Authentic Yoga for beings
is certainly according to the order of things.
In the fulfillment of *dharma*, the fruit that is obtained
is the appropriate consequence of the thought of beings.

CONCLUDING REMARKS (VERSES 222–228)

kulādiyoginām asmān matto'pi jaḍadhīmatām
śravaṇāt pakṣapātāder upakāro'sti leśataḥ

222. For the Family Yogins,
who are drunken and more stupid than us,

might side with our case from hearing this
and derive some small benefit.

tāttvikaḥ pakṣapātaś ca bhāvaśūnyā ca yā kriyā
anayor antaraṃ jñeyaṃ bhānukhadyotayor iva

223. Siding with the true teaching,
but with actions that are empty of the mood,
there is a difference between these two
like that between the sun and a firefly.

khadyotakasya yat tejas tad alpaṃ ca vināśi ca
viparītam idam bhānor iti bhāvyam idaṃ budhaiḥ

224. The light of a firefly is small and waning,
while that of the sun is the opposite.
This is to be understood by the wise.

śravaṇe prārthanīyāḥ syur na hi yogayāh kadācana
yatnaḥ kalyāṇasattvānāṃ mahāratne sthito yataḥ

225. Those pleasant persons
make an effort at hearing [such a text];
they stand firm in the great jewel.

naitadvidas tv ayogyebhyo dadaty enaṃ tathāpi tu
haribhadra idaṃ prāha naitebhyo deya ādarāt

226. The wise ones do not give this
to those who are unsuitable;
Haribhadra says it is not to be given to them
out of respect.

avajñeha kṛtālpāpi yad anarthāya jāyate
atas tatparihārārthaṃ na punar bhāvadoṣataḥ

227. The contempt that is engendered in this case is unfortunate,
and very little is gained.
Rather, it is due to [the purification of] letting go
that faults truly cease to recur.

yogyebhyas tu prayatnena deyo'yaṃ vidhinānvitaiḥ
mātsaryavirahenoccaiḥ śreyovighnapraśāntaye

228. This is to be given to the suitable ones who are established in the law through great effort,
along with those lofty ones who have abandoned envy
for the sake of removing impediments to true blessedness.

Notes

PREFACE

1. See Eric Konigsberg, "The Yuppie Guru's Last Seduction," *New York* (July 20, 1998): pp. 20–28, for a journalistic account of this tragedy.

CHAPTER ONE

1. R. S. Shukla, *India as Known to Haribhadra Suri* (Meerut: Kusumanjali Prakashan, 1989), 1.
2. R. Williams, "Haribhadra," *Bulletin of the School of Oriental and African Studies, University of London* 28 (1965): 101–11. In light of this particular study, Williams even suggests that the Haribhadra who wrote the *Yogadṛṣṭisamuccaya,* differs from the HB who wrote the *Yogabindu*, attributing the former to the later Haribhadra, to whom Williams refers as "Yakini-putra," and the latter, the *Yogabindu*, to the original author, who flourished in the sixth century (102–103). A comparative reading of the two texts finds virtually no reference to the Patañjali Yoga tradition in the *Yogabindu*, whereas the *Yogadṛṣṭisamuccaya* concerns itself almost exclusively with Patañjali's eightfold path and a comparative study of Yoga in the face of competition from Tantra, Buddhism, and Vedānta. The *Yogabindu* contains a more overtly Jaina terminology, while the *Yogadṛṣṭisamuccaya,* as we will see, minimizes its Jaina content. In particular, the *Yogabindu*, while initially giving praise to the final goal of the Vedānta, Buddhism, and Sāṃkhya, concentrates on the explication of five steps of yoga, summarized by Nathmal Tatia as follows: "*adhyātma* or contemplation of truth accompanied by moral conduct, *bhāvanā* or repeated practice in the contemplation accompanied by steadfastness of the mind, *dhyāna* or concentration of the mind, *samatā* or equanimity, and *vṛttisaṃkṣaya* or annhilation of all the traces of *karman*" (see Nathmal Tatia, *Studies in Jaina Philosophy* [Banaras: Jain Cultural Research Society, 1951], 297). Also the *Yogadṛṣṭisamuccaya* concerns itself with Tantra, a prominent movement in the eighth century; Tantra receives virtually no attention in the *Yogabindu*, which might be attributed to its possible earlier date.

3. See Suvrat Muni Shastri, *Jaina Yoga in Light of the Yogabindu (An Analytical Study)* (Delhi: Nirmal, 1996), 45–51; Shukla, *India as Known to Haribhadra Suri*, 6–12, for summaries of both Indian and Western scholarship on this issue.

4. Yajneshwar S. Shastri, *Acārya Umāsvāti Vācaka's Praśamaratiprakaraṇa Critically Edited with English Translation* (Ahmedabad: L. D. Institute of Indology, 1989), Introduction.

5. Phyllis Granoff, "Jain Lives of Haribhadra: An Inquiry into the Sources and Logic of the Legends," *Journal of Indian Philosophy* 17:2 (1989): 111–12. Granoff also mentions that Haribhadra describes a similar Brahmin in his own writing. See page 113.

6. These nephews seem to be styled after two Jaina brothers, Akalaṅka and Niṣkalaṅka, whose story is told in the *Kathākośa* (1077 C.E.) two centuries before a variant story about Haribhadra occurs in the *Prabhāvakacarita*. In the *Kathākośa*, the two brothers are put to a Buddhist loyalty test, fail, and beat a hasty escape. Niṣkalaṅka is captured and put to death. Akalaṅka is sheltered by a Jaina queen and bests the Buddhist goddess, Tārā, in debate (Granoff, "Jain Lives," 114). The Haribhadra story, which occurs in several accounts, changes the names of the brothers to Haṃsa and Paramahaṃsa. In the *Purātanaprabandhasaṃgraha*, Haribhadra does not encourage the two students to enter the monastery. In this account, Haṃsa dies fighting Buddhist soldiers, and Paramahaṃsa is killed after losing a debate. A bird takes Paramahaṃsa's bloodied, path-clearing broom to Haribhadra, who, in a rage, "makes a cauldron of boiling oil and magically causes the Buddhists to fly through the sky and land in his boiling pot, where they [700 Buddhists] are scalded to death" (ibid., 117). The mayhem stops when one of Haribhadra's students, sent by the teacher Jinabhadra, interrupts this process. According to this early version of the story, Haribhadra, having already written his many important books, then composes his final treatise, the *Samarāiccakahā*. Out of continuing despair (which would not be acceptable within the Jaina faith), he then fasts to death. For a complete investigation of these stories, see the excellent and intriguing article by Granoff, cited above.

7. No such king is mentioned in the historical records.

8. See Padmanabh S. Jaini, *The Jaina Path of Purification* (Berkeley: University of California Press, 1979), 275, 285, 304. Granoff suggests that the reason that Haribhadra so wanted to distinguish Jainism from Buddhism lay in the fact that as Jainas sought patronage from Hindu kings, it might have been beneficial to clearly separate their own tradition from that of Buddhism, which had waned and become unpopular by the tenth or eleventh century. See the article by Granoff, cited above, p. 123. See also Jaini's article, "The Disappearance of Buddhism and the Survival of Jainism in India: A Study in Contrast," in *Collected Papers on Buddhist Studies* (Delhi: Motilal Banarsidass, 2001), 139–53, where he atttibutes Jaina survival to the strength of the Jaina laity and the willingness of the Jainas to adopt devotional practices similar to Hindu *bhakti*, as seen in their recasting of Ṛṣabha as an *avatāra* and the development of Jaina versions of the *Rāmāyaṇa* and the *Mahābhārata*.

9. H. R. Kapadia, ed. *Anekāntajayapatākā*, vol. 1 (Baroda: Oriental Institute, 1940), 27, 29.

10. Shukla, *India as Known*, 7–10.

11. This is abbreviated from Friedhelm Hardy's summary translation based on the *Bṛhatkathākośa* in Phyllis Granoff, ed., *The Clever Adulteress and Other Stories: A Treasury of Jaina Literature* (Oakville, Ont.: Mosaic Press, 1990), 118–39. The last quote is from verse 305, as translated by Hardy in Granoff, *The Clever Adulteress*, 132.

12. Granoff, "Jain Lives of Haribhadra," 108.

13. M. Sivakumara Swamy, *Haribhadra's Sad-Darśana-Samuccaya* (Bangalore: Bangalore University, 1977). Olle Qvarnstrom has provided a comprehensive study of Haribhadra's doxographies as well as a new translation of the *Ṣaḍdarśanasamuccaya* in his article, "Haribhadra and the Beginning of Doxography in India," in *Approaches to Jaina Studies: Philosophy, Logic, Rituals, and Symbols,* ed. N. K. Wagle and Olle Qvarnstrom (Toronto: University of Toronto Center for South Asian Studies, 1999), 169–210.

14. Paul Dundas, *The Jains* (London: Routledge, 1992), 197. The many-pointed doctrine (*anekānta*) has been extensively discussed in literature on Jaina philosophy. See, in particular, Bimal Krishna Matilal, *The Central Philosophy of Jainism (Anekanta Vada)* (Ahmedabad: L. D. Institute of Indology, 1981). Also, for a comprehensive and critical assessment of "many-sidedness," see John Cort, "Intellectual *Ahiṃsā* Revisited: Jain Tolerance and Intolerance of Others," *Philosophy East and West* 50:3 (July 2000): 324–47.

15. I have suggested elsewhere that the story of Buddhists boiled in oil most likely was in response to the political and social climate of India when the stories were recorded, 500 years after the death of Haribhadra. See Tara Sethia, ed., "Religious Dissonance and Reconciliation: The Haribhadra Story," *The Lessons of Ahimsa and Anekantada for Contemporary Life* (Pomona: California State Polytechnic University, 2002).

16. See note fourteen. See also my chapter, "Nonviolent Approaches to Multiplicity," in *Nonviolence to Animals, Earth, and Self in Asian Traditions* (Albany: State University of New York Press, 1993), 85–97.

17. Granoff, "Jain Lives of Haribhadra," 107.

18. Shastri suggests that because Umāsvāti exhibits the same familiarity with Sāṃkhya, Yoga, and Nyāya, as found in the Buddhist works of Vasubandhu, he was probably his contemporary. See Shastri, *Acārya,* 3.

19. For more detailed information on early meditation in these traditions, see Johannes Bronkhorst, *The Two Traditions of Meditation in Ancient India* (Delhi: Motilal Banarsidass, 1993), and Will J. Johnson, *Harmless Souls: Karmic Bondage and Religious Change in Early Jainism, with Special Reference to Umāsvāti and Kundakunda* (Delhi: Motilal Banarsidass, 1995). See also Johnson's article, "Kundakunda: Two-standpoints and the *Anekāntavāda*," in *Approaches to Jaina Studies*, ed. N. K. Wagle and Olle Qvarnstrom, 101–12.

20. Indukala Jhavari, "Introduction," in *Haribhadrasūri's Yogaśataka with Auto-Commentary along with His Brahmasiddhāntasamuccaya*, ed. Munirāja

Śri Puṇyavijayajī (Ahmedabad: Lalbhai Dalpatbhai Bharatiya Sanskriti Vidyamandira, 1965), 18.

21. Shastri, *Jaina Yoga in the Light of the Yogabindu*, 77.

CHAPTER TWO

1. These include friendliness toward the virtuous, compassion for those suffering, happiness toward the meritorious, and equanimity toward the evil ones (*YS* I:33).

2. I am grateful to Arvind Sharma for this reference, pursuant to our conversation of January 18, 2001.

3. Padmanabh S. Jaini, *The Jaina Path of Purification* (Berkeley: University of California Press, 1979), 5.

4. For more on the history of Jainism, see the writings of Padmanabh S. Jaini and Paul Dundas. For a modern translation of the *Tattvārtha Sūtra*, see Nathmal Tatia, *That Which Is: The Tattvārtha Sūtra of Umāsvāti* (San Francisco: HarperCollins, 1994).

5. Yajneshwar S. Shastri, *Acārya Umāsvati Vācaka's Praśamaratiprakaraṇa Critically Edited with English Translation* (Ahmedabad: L. D. Institute of Indology, 1989), 34.

6. See *Praśamaratiprakaraṇa*, verse 277, in Shastri, *Acārya*, 64.

7. Jaini, *The Jaina Path*, 148.

8. Ibid., 157.

9. Muni Shri Nyayavijayaji, *Jaina Philosophy and Religion*, trans. Nagin J. Shah (Delhi: Motilal Banarsidass, 1998), 70.

10. Tatia, *That Which Is*, 282.

11. Helmut von Glasenapp, *Jainism: An Indian Religion of Salvation*, trans. Shridhar B. Shrotri (Delhi: Motilal Banarsidass, 1999), 223.

12. Tatia, *That Which Is*, 283.

13. Ibid., 284.

14. See Padmanabh S. Jaini, *Gender and Salvation: Jaina Debates on the Spiritual Liberation of Women* (Berkeley: University of California Press, 1991), for a discussion of gender issues in the Jaina tradition. For a discussion of the interchangeability of sexual emotions, see Robert P. Goldman's Foreword, p. xviii.

15. Tatia, *That Which Is*, 284.

16. Ibid.

17. Jaini, *The Jaina Path of Purification*, 159.

18. Tatia, *That Which Is*, p. 284.

19. Ibid., 285.

20. Jaini, *The Jaina Path of Purification*, 159.

21. Von Glasenapp, *Jainism*, 93.

22. Dr. Pravin L. Shah has developed an alternate correlation. He surmises that one remains in the first *guṇasthāna* during all four beginning phases

of Haribhadra's system, though one begins to develop a spiritual longing. In Haribhadra's fifth phase (Sthirā), one leaps into a state of awareness that correlates to the fourth *guṇasthāna* (*samyakdṛṣṭi*). In the sixth (Kāntā), one oscillates between the fourth and seventh *guṇasthānas*; in the seventh (Prabhā), one rises to the twelfth. In the eighth (Parā), one achieves the final two phases of *sayoga kevala* (thirteen) and *ayoga kevala*, or liberation (fourteen) (personal correspondence, July 2001).

Pandit Dhirajlal Mehta of Surat, Gujarat, states that one attains the fourth *guṇasthāṇa* in Haribhadra's fifth phase (Sthirā), attains *guṇasthānas* five through seven in the sixth (Kāntā), *guṇasthānas* eight through ten in the seventh (Prabhā), and, skipping over the troublesome eleventh *guṇasthāna*, reaches the top three *guṇasthānas* in Haribhadra's Parā or Highest Yoga. [Personal conversation June 2002, facilitated by Sushma Parekh). Neither of these scholars agrees with my interpretation of the term *apūrvakaraṇa*.

CHAPTER THREE

1. The verse numbers and the names attributed to Haribhadra, Bhagavaddatta, Bhāskara, and Patanjali, respectively, are as follows: 16 and 21 (1. Mitrā or Friendly, *adveṣa* or no aversion, *akheda* or no distress, and *yama* or restraint); 41 (2. Tārā or Protector, *jijñāsā* or desirous of knowledge, *anudvega* or free from anxiety, and *niyama* or observances); 49, 52–53 for Bhagavaddatta (3. Balā or Power, *śuśrūṣā* or desirous to hear truth), 55–56 for Bhāskara (3. *akṣepa* or no distraction, and *āsana* or Yoga postures in Patañjali); 57, 60–62 (4. Dīprā or Shining, *śravaṇa* or hearing truth, *anuttānavatī* or no interruption, and *prāṇāyāma* or breath control); 154, extending in general terms through 159 (5. Shtirā or Firm, *sūkṣmabodha* or subtle awakening, *abhrānti* or unmuddied, and *pratyāhāra* or sense withdrawal/inwardness); 162, extending in general terms through 168 (6. Kāntā or Pleasing, *mīmāṃsā* or reflection, *ananyamud* or not finding pleasure in the other, and *dhāraṇā* or concentration); 170, extending in general terms through 174 (7. Prabhā or Radiant, *pratipatti* or perception of truth, *arug* or without pain, and *dhyāna* or meditation); 178, extending in general terms through 186 (8. Parā or Highest, *sātmī-kṛta-pravṛtti* or enactment of absorption, *saṅga vivarjitā* or free from attachment, and *samādhi*).

2. Paṇḍit Sukhalala Sanghavi, *Samadarśī Acārya Haribhadra* (Bombay: Mumbai University, 1961), 80.

3. Srinivasa Murthy, trans., *The Bhagavad Gītā* (Long Beach: Long Beach Publishing, 1985), 43, 57.

4. Y. S. Shastri has suggested that although he does not use the direct terminology of Asaṅga, Bhāskara seems to allude to the concept of the ten Yogabhūmis. See Shastri's book, *Mahāyānasūtrālankāra of Asaṅga: A Study in Vijñānavāda Buddhism* (Delhi: Indian Books Center, 1989), 115–17.

5. Commentary on verse 21, Haribhadra, *Yogadṛṣṭisamuccaya* (Ahmedabad: Jain Grantha Prakashaka Sabha, 1940b).

6. Ibid., commentary on verse 154.

CHAPTER FOUR

1. Swami Venkatesananda, trans., *The Concise Yogavāsiṣṭha* (Albany: State University of New York Press, 1984), 249.

2. *The Yogavāsiṣṭha of Vālmīki,* Vol. I. English translation, Vihari Lal Mitra, revised by Ravi Prakash Arya. Delhi: Parimal Publications, 1998. III:5:7, p. 167.

3. Ibid., Vol. II, V:72:41, p. 457.

4. Paul Dundas, *The Jains* (London: Routledge, 1992), 196.

5. Christopher Key Chapple and Yogi Ananda Viraj (Eugene P. Kelly Jr.), trans. *The Yoga Sūtras of Patañjali: An Analysis of the Sanskrit with Accompanying English Translation* (Delhi: Sri Satguru, 1990), 62–63.

6. The *Mādhyamika-śāstra* of Nāgārjuna, trans. Th. Stcherbatsky in *The Conception of Buddhist Nirvāṇa* (Leningrad: Academy of Sciences of the USSR, 1927), pp. 69–78.

CHAPTER FIVE

1. Christopher Key Chapple, "Reading Patañjali without Vyāsa," *Journal of the American Academy of Religion* LXII (1994): 85–105.

2. Winthrop Sargeant, trans., *Bhagavad Gītā* (Albany: State University of New York Press, 1994), II:64.

3. Georg Feuerstein and Jeanine Miller, *The Essence of Yoga* (Rochester, Vermont: Inner Traditions, 1998), 14.

4. *Yoga Sūtra* III:23 states "[By *saṃyama*, the combined application of concentration, meditation, and *samādhi*] on friendliness and so forth, [corresponding] powers arise."

5. See *Yoga Sūtra* III:35: "When there is no distinction of intention between the pure *puruṣa* and the perfect *sattva*, there is experience for the purpose of the other (*puruṣa*); from *saṃyama* on purpose being for the self, there is knowledge of *puruṣa*."

6. Georg Feuerstein, *Holy Madness: The Shock Tactics and Radical Teachings of Crazy-Wise Adepts, Holy Fools, and Rascal Gurus* (New York: Paragon, 1991), 5–6.

7. Jerome Bauer writes: "Jaini compares Hindu, Buddhist, and Jaina concepts of *śubha*, *śuddha*, and *maṅgala*. *Śubha* refers to the worldly pure, *śuddha* to the transcendentally pure. *Maṅgala*, the auspicious, was originally reserved for activity relating to the first three Hindu ends of life. . . . *Śuddha*, the transcendentally pure, was reserved for activities relating to . . . *mokṣa*." See Jerome Bauer, "Karma and Control: The Prodigious and the Auspicious in Śvetāmbara Jaina Canonical Mythology" (Ph.D. diss., University of Pennsylvania, 1998), 489–90. Jaini himself writes that "the Buddhists and the Jainas attempted to assimilate the ascetic ideal into *maṅgala*, not by degrading the *śuddha*, but instead raising *maṅgala* to a new status which incorporated both the worldly *śubha* and the supermundane *śuddha*, relegating all activities not

conducive to salvation to the category of *aśuddha*." See P. S. Jaini, *Collected Papers on Jain Studies* (Delhi: Motilal Banarsidass, 2000), 238. Haribhadra does not seem to make a distinction between these two terms.

CHAPTER SIX

1. See Katherine Anne Harper and Robert L. Brown, eds. *The Roots of Tantra* (Albany: State University of New York Press, 2002), for a detailed history of the origins of Tantra.

2. See Paul Dundas, "Becoming Gautama: Mantra and History in Śvetāmbara Jainism" in *Open Boundaries: Jain Communities and Cultures in Indian History,* ed. John Cort (Albany: State University of New York Press, 1998), 31–52, and his "The Jain Monk Jinapati Sūri Gets the Better of a Nāth Yogī," in *Tantra in Practice,* ed. David Gordon White (Princeton: Princeton University Press, 2000), pp. 231–38. See also John Cort, "Worship of Bell-Ears the Great Hero, a Jain Tantric Deity," in White, pp. 417–33, and Olle Qvarnstrom, "Jain Tantra: Divinatory and Meditative Practices in the Twelfth-Century *Yogaśāstra* of Hemacandra," in White, pp. 595–604.

3. John Cort, "Medieval Jaina Goddesses," *Numen* 34 (1987), Fasc. 2.

4. Vidya Dehejia, *Yoginī Cult and Temples: A Tantric Tradition* (New Delhi: National Museum, 1986), 185.

5. Lina Gupta, trans., "Tantric Incantation in the *Devī Purāṇa: Padamālā Mantra Vidyā,*" in *The Roots of Tantra*, ed. Harper and Brown, 234–35.

6. I differ here with the interpretation of S. M. Desai, who equates *avedyasaṃvedya* with Patañjali's first five outer limbs (*bahiranga*) and *vedyasaṃvedya* with the inner limbs (*antaraṅga*) of *dhāraṇā, dhyāna*, and *samādhi.* See his *Haribhadra's Yoga Works and Psychosynthesis* (Ahmedabad: L. D. Institute of Indology, 1983), 59. As noted earlier, Bhatt's commentary on the Laws of Manu, X, 24, uses the term to describe prohibited sexual behavior.

7. Dirtiness (*mālinyam*) bears close similarity to the name "Malinī," an epithet for the goddess, Durgā.

8. See Douglas Renfrew Brooks's excerpted translation of the *Kulārṇava Tantra* (ca. 1000–1400 C.E.), "The Ocean of the Heart: Selections from the *Kulārṇava Tantra,*" in *Tantra in Practice*, ed. David Gordon White, pp. 347–60. Brooks writes that the goal of Tantra is to "enable the committed disciple to transform his or her own life into a life of joy and liberation. Thus, the Tantra commends the twin goals of human existence, bhukti, worldly enjoyment, and mukti, ultimate liberation, as its promise to those who keep its secrets and take up its disciplines. The Kula path, it goes on to say, is the sole path that can promise both of these aims in this very lifetime; it is therefore superior to all others. One becomes capable of enjoyment only to the degree that one is advancing toward liberation; similarly, the liberated are the only ones who experience life's true enjoyment" (p. 350).

9. See Douglas Renfrew Brooks, *The Secret of the Three Cities: An Introduction to Hindu Śākta Tantrism* (Chicago: University of Chicago Press, 1990). Though the texts discussing the three cities were composed after

Haribhadra, Haribhadra's *Yogadṛṣṭisamuccaya* might provide an early version of this idea. See also Y. S. Shastri's essay, "Tripura Tantra (Sri Vidya): Its Philosophy and Path of Sadhana," in his *Traverses on the Less Trodden Path of Indian Philosophy and Religion* (Ahmedabad: L. D. Institute of Indology, 1991), 141–60. Shastri translated these three as "will power, knowledge, and action." Pandit Sukhalala Sanghavi, in *Samadarsī Acārya Haribhadra* (Bombay: Mumbai University, 1961), states that Desire (*icchā*) is like inclination (*adhimukha*) or attraction. Instruction (*jñāna*) is the inculcation of metaphysical principles in one's life through the precepts of the Yogis. Effort (*kriyā*) is based on one's own experience and enthusiasm (*utsaha*).

10. As cited in R. Antnathakrishna Sastry, trans., *Lalitā-Sahasranāma with Bhāskarāya's Commentary* (Madras: Adyar Library and Research Center, 1899), 187.

11. Ibid., 158. Ambikā also is the name of a Jaina goddess.

12. Ibid., 259.

13. Ibid., 266.

14. Ibid., 23.

15. Ibid., 154.

16. Dehejia, *Yoginī Cult and Temples*, 197.

17. Ibid., 215.

18. Ibid., 215.

19. Sanjukta Gupta, trans., *Lakṣmī Tantra: A Pāñcarātra Text* (Delhi: Motilal Banarsidass, 2000), p. 290.

20. Sir John Woodroffe, *The Garland of Letters: Studies in the Mantra-Śāstra* (Pondicherry: Ganesh and Company, 1979), 217.

21. Katherine Anne Harper, *The Iconography of the Saptamātṛkas: Seven Hindu Goddesses of Spiritual Transformation* (Lewiston: Edwin Mellen Press, 1989), pp. 73–100.

22. See Dehejia, *Yoginī Cult and Temples*, 34.

23. Mohanlal Bhagavantas Jhavery attributes an earlier date to the *Kulārṇava Tantra* than does Douglas Renfrew Brooks, who places it between the tenth and fourteenth centuries. See Jhavery, *Comparative and Critical Study of Mantraśāstra* (Ahmedabad: Sarabhai Manilal Nawals, 1944); Brooks, "The Ocean of the Heart: Selections from the *Kulārṇava Tantra*," in *Tantra in Practice*, ed. David Gordon White, p. 347.

24. Cort, "Medieval Jaina Goddesses," 237.

25. Jhavery, *Comparative*, 176, 260.

26. Cort, "Medieval Jaina Goddesses," 239.

27. Ibid.

28. Jhavery, *Comparative*, 298.

29. K. K. Handiqui, *Yaśastilaka and Indian Culture* (Solapur: Jaina Samskriti Samrakasaka Sangha, 1949), pp. 199–216.

CHAPTER SEVEN

1. The *Bhagavad Gītā* includes a similar ranking of four types of spiritual seekers. The first type is quite savvy; the second has had a secondhand

experience; the third has heard about it; and the fourth group does not understand even the fundamentals of spiritual life. Swami Prabhavananda and Christopher Isherwood translate this passage as follows: "There are some who have actually looked upon the Atman, and understood It, in all Its wonder. Others can only speak of It as wonderful beyond their understanding. Others know of Its wonder by hearsay. And there are others who are told about It and do not understand a word" (II:29). From *The Song of God: Bhagavad-Gita* (New York: New American Library, 1944), 88.

2. In his study of Bhāskararāya's commentary on the *Tripurā Upaniṣad*, Brooks notes that the author "views the feminine principle as the creative center, one whose nature is to initiate action. He repeats this general concept . . . when he explains how divinity actually assumes the shape of the manifest universe . . . Śakti appears as will (*icchā*), knowledge (*jñāna*), and action (*kriyā*)." See Douglas Renfrew Brooks, *The Secret of the Three Cities: An Introduction to Hindu Śākta Tantrism* (Chicago: University of Chicago Press, 1990), 97.

3. See Lawrence A. Babb, *Absent Lord: Ascetics and Kings in a Jain Ritual Culture* (Berkeley: University of California Press, 1996), 26–30, 61–63, 72–82, 84–91.

4. "It is affirmed by the [Svetambara] SB/SBT tradition [Umāsvāti's *Svopajña Bhāṣya* and Siddhasenagaṇi's *Svopajña Bhāṣya Ṭīka* commentaries on the *Tattvārthasūtra*] that physical gender—female, male, or hermaphroditic—and dress have no bearing on attaining liberation. Even a householder wearing their daily garb can be liberated." Commentary on *Tattvārthasūtra,* 10.7, in Nathmal Tatia, trans., *That Which Is: The Tattvārtha Sūtra of Umāsvāti* (San Francisco: HarperCollins, 1994), 257.

5. Lawrence A. Babb notes that these "beings are worthy of worship, and it is crucial to note that these are the *only* entities the tradition deems fully worthy of worship. They are, in order, the *arhats* ("worthy ones" who have attained omniscience; the Tirthankars), the *siddhas* (the liberated), the *ācāryas* (ascetic leaders), the *upādhyāyas* (ascetic preceptors), and the *sādhus* (ordinary ascetics). . . . These beings, we see, are all ascetics. This is the fundamental matter: Jains worship ascetics." See Babb, *Absent Lord,* 22–23.

6. Georg Feuerstein, *Holy Madness: The Shock Tactics and Radical Teachings of Crazy-Wise Adepts, Holy Fools, and Rascal Gurus* (New York: Paragon, 1991), 192.

7. According to Padmanabh S. Jaini, "The Jaina tradition unanimously believes that the mendicant Jambū was the last person to attain mokṣa in the current time. He was the disciple of Sudharman, one of the two gaṇadharas . . . who survived Mahāvīra. Jambu is believed to have died in 463 B.C.E., sixty-four years after the nirvāṇa of Mahāvīra. Jainas are unanimous in their belief that mokṣa cannot be attained by anyone, whether a monk or a nun until the present time cycle is completed and a new era begins and a new Jina appears here (after a lapse of several thousands [of] years)." See Padmanabh S. Jaini, *Gender and Salvation: Jaina Debates on the Spiritual Liberation of Women* (Berkeley: University of California Press, 1991), 98.

8. Ortega y Gasset, Jose, *Meditations on Quixote* (Chicago: University of Illinois Press, 2000), p. 45.

YOGADṚṢṬISAMUCCAYA (A COLLECTION OF VIEWS ON YOGA)

1. K. K. Dixit, *The Yogabindu of Ācārya Haribhadrasūri* (Ahmedabad: Lalbhai Dalpatbhai Bharatiya Sanskriti Vidyamandira, 1968), p. 8.

2. See Chapple, "Reading Patañjali without Vyāsa: A Critique of Four *Yoga Sūtra* Passages," *Journal of the American Academy of Religion* 62 (1994): 1.

3. Dixit, *Yogabindu,* p. 8.

4. S. M. Desai, *Haribhadra's Yoga Works and Psychosynthesis* (Ahmedabad: L. D. Institute of Indology, 1983), p. 59.

5. See Nathmal Tatia, trans. *That Which Is: Tattvārtha Sūtra* (San Francisco: HarperCollins, 1994), p. 282 and Helmut von Glasenapp, *Jainism: An Indian Religion of Salvation,* translated by Shridhar B. Shrotri. (Delhi: Motilal Banarsidass, 1999), pp. 222–223.

6. See Tatia, *That Which Is,* pp. 283–284.

7. Haribhadra repeats his theme here that the beginning forms of Yoga (Mitrā, Tārā, Balā, Diprā) are like the light from fires of grass, cowdung, wood, and an oil lamp, while the more advanced forms (Sthirā, Kāntā, Prabhā, Parā) are more enduring and powerful, like a shining jewel, a star, lightning, and the moon. This does not correlate to Patañjali's distinction between the five outer limbs (*bahiraṅga*) of disciplines, observances, postures, breath control, and detachment as contrasted with the three inner limbs (*antaraṅga*) of concentration, meditation, and *samādhi.* Haribhadra does not make any allusions to the *guṇasthānas* on this verse.

8. Dixit has chosen *upajāyate* ("arises") here, while the ms. of the Jain Grantha Prakashaka Sabha (1940b) shows the variant *upapadyate* ("approaches"), entailing no great difference in meaning within the context of Haribhadra's discussion.

Bibliography

Babb Lawrence A. *Absent Lord: Ascetics and Kings in a Jain Ritual Culture.* Berkeley: University of California Press, 1996.

Bauer, Jerome. "Karma and Control: The Prodigious and the Auspicious in Śvetāmbara Jaina Canonical Mythology." Ph.D. diss., University of Pennsylvania, 1998.

Bronkhorst, Johannes. *The Two Traditions of Meditation in Ancient India.* Delhi: Motilal Banarsidass, 1993.

Brooks, Douglas Renfrew. *The Secret of the Three Cities: An Introduction to Hindu Śākta Tantrism.* Chicago: University of Chicago Press, 1990.

Chapple, Christopher Key. *Karma and Creativity.* Albany: State University of New York Press, 1986.

———. *Nonviolence to Animals, Earth, and Self in Asian Traditions.* Albany: State University of New York Press, 1993.

———. "Reading Patañjali without Vyāsa: A Critique of Four *Yoga Sūtra* Passages." *Journal of the American Academy of Religion* 62 (1994): 85–105.

Chapple, Christopher Key, and Yogi Ananda Viraj (Eugene P. Kelly Jr.), translators. *The Yoga Sūtras of Patañjali: An Analysis of the Sanskrit with Accompanying English Translation.* Delhi: Sri Satguru, 1990.

Cort, John. "Medieval Jaina Goddesses." *Numen* 34(1987): Fasc. 2.

———. "Intellectual *Ahiṃsā* Revisited: Jain Tolerance and Intolerance of Others." *Philosophy East and West* 50:3 (July 2000): 324–47.

———, ed. *Open Boundaries: Jain Communities and Cultures in Indian History.* Albany: State University of New York Press, 1998.

Dass, Baba Ram. *Remember Be Here Now.* San Cristobal, New Mexico: Lam Foundation, 1971.

Dehejia, Vidya. *Yoginī Cult and Temples: A Tantric Tradition.* New Delhi: National Museum, 1986.

Desai, S. M. *Haribhadra's Yoga Works and Psychosynthesis.* Ahmedabad: L. D. Institute of Indology, 1983.

Dixit, K. K., trans. *The Yogabindu of Acārya Haribhadrasuri.* Ahmedabad: Lalbhai Dalpatbhai Bharatiya Sanskriti Vidyamandira, 1968.

———, trans. *Yogadṛṣṭisamuccaya and Yogaviṃśika of Acārya Haribhadrasuri.* Ahmedabad: Lalbhai Dalpatbhai Bharatiya Sanskriti Vidyamandira, 1970.

Dundas, Paul. *The Jains.* London: Routledge, 1992.

Eliade, Mircea. *Yoga: Immortality and Freedom.* Princeton: Princeton University Press, 1969.

Feuerstein, Georg. *Holy Madness: The Shock Tactics and Radical Teachings of Crazy-Wise Adepts, Holy Fools, and Rascal Gurus.* New York: Paragon, 1991.

———. *The Yoga Tradition: Its History, Literature, Philosophy, and Practice.* Prescott: Hohm Press, 1998.

Feuerstein, Georg, and Jeanine Miller. *The Essence of Yoga.* Rochester, VT: Inner Traditions, 1998.

Glasenapp, Helmut von. *Jainism: An Indian Religion of Salvation.* Translated by Shridhar B. Shrotri. Delhi: Motilal Banarsidass, 1999.

Granoff, Phyllis. "Jain Lives of Haribhadra: An Inquiry into the Sources and Logic of the Legends." *Journal of Indian Philosophy* 17:2 (1989): 105–28.

———, ed. *The Clever Adulteress and Other Stories: A Treasury of Jain Literature.* Oakville, Ont. Mosaic Press, 1990.

Gupta, Sanjukta, trans. *Lakṣmī Tantra: A Pāñcarātra Text.* Delhi: Motilal Banarsidass, 2000.

Handiqui, K. K. *Yaśastilaka and Indian Culture.* Solapur: Jaina Samskrit Samrakasaka Sangha, 1949.

Haribhadra. *Yogabindu.* Ahmedabad: Jain Grantha Prakashaka Sabha, 1940a.

———. *Yogadṛṣṭisamuccaya.* Ahmedabad: Jain Grantha Prakashaka Sabha, 1940b.

———. *Haribhadrasūri's Yogaśataka with Autocommentary along with His Brahmasiddhāntasamuccaya.* Edited by Munirāja Śri Puṇyavijayajī. Ahmedabad: Lalbhai Dalpatbhai Bharatiya Sankriti Vidyamandira, 1965.

Harper, Katherine Anne. *The Iconography of the Saptamātṛkas: Seven Hindu Goddesses of Spiritual Transformation.* Lewiston: Edwin Mellen Press, 1989.

Harper, Katherine Anne, and Robert L. Brown, eds. *The Roots of Tantra.* Albany: State University of New York Press, 2002.

Isherwood Christopher and Swami Prabhavananda. *How to Know God.* New York: Mentor Books.

Jaini, Padmanabh S. *The Jaina Path of Purification.* Berkeley: Univeristy of California Press, 1979.

———. *Gender and Salvation: Jaina Debates on the Spiritual Liberation of Women.* Berkeley: University of California Press, 1991.

———. *Collected Papers on Jaina Studies.* Delhi: Motilal Banarsidass, 2000.

———. *Collected Papers on Buddhist Studies.* Delhi: Motilal Banarsidass, 2001.

Jhavery, Mohanlal Bhagavantas. *Comparative and Critical Study of Mantraśāstra.* Ahmedabad: Sarabhai Manilal Nawals, 1944.

Johnson, Will J. *Harmless Souls: Karmic Bondage and Religious Change in Early Jainism, with Special Reference to Umāsvāti and Kundakunda.* Delhi: Motilal Banarsidass, 1995.

Kapadia, H. R., ed. *Anekāntajayapatākā by Haribhadra Suri* (in Sanskrit). 2 vols. Baroda: Oriental Institute, 1940, 1947.

Matilal, Bimal Krishna. *The Central Philosophy of Jainism (Anekanta Vada).* Ahmedabad: L. D. Institute of Indology, 1981.

Murthy, Srinivasa, trans. *The Bhagavad Gītā.* Long Beach: Long Beach Publishing, 1985.

Nyayavijayaji, Muni Shri. *Jaina Philosophy and Religion.* Translated by Nagin J. Shah. Delhi: Motilal Banarsidass, 1998.

Prabhavananda, Swami and Christopher Isherwood, trans. *The Song of God: Bhagavad Gita.* New York: New American Library, 1944.

———. *How to Know God.* New York: New American Library, 1953.

Sanghavi, Pandit Sukhalala. *Samadarśi Ācārya Haribhadra.* Bombay: Mumbai University, 1961.

Sargeant, Winthrop, trans. *Bhagavad Gītā.* Albany: State University of New York Press, 1994.

Sastry, R. Antnathakrishna, trans. *Lalitā-Sahasranāma with Bhākarāya's Commentary.* Madras: Adyar Library and Research Center, 1899.

Stcherbatsky, Th. *The Conception of Buddhist Nirvāna.* Leningrad: Academy of Sciences of the USSR, 1927.

Senart, Emile. "Bouddhisme et Yoga." *La Revue de l'Historie des Religions* 42 (1900): 345–64.

Sethia, Tara, ed. *The Lessons of Ahiṃsā and Anekānta for Contemporary Life*. Pomona: California State Polytechnic University, 2002.

Shastri, Suvrat Muni. *Jaina Yoga in Light of the Yogabindu (An Analytical Study)*. Delhi: Nirmal, 1996.

Shastri, Yajneshwar S. *Acārya Umāsvāti Vācaka's Praśamaratiprakaraṇa Critically Edited with English Translation*. Ahmedabad: L. D. Institute of Indology, 1989a.

———. *Mahāyānasūtrālaṅkāra of Asaṅga: A Study in Vijñāñavāda Buddhism*. Delhi: Indian Books Center, 1989b.

———. *Traverses on the Less Trodden Path of Indian Philosophy and Religion*. Ahmedabad: L. D. Institute of Indology, 1991.

Shukla, R. S. *India as Known to Haribhadra Suri*. Meerut: Kusumanjali Prakashan, 1989.

Suali, Luigi, ed. *Haribhadra's Yogadṛṣṭisamuccaya*. Bhavanagar: Jaina Dharma Prasaraka Sabha, 1911.

Swamy, M. Sivakumara. *Haribhadra's Sad-Darśana-Samuccaya*. Bangalore: Bangalore University, 1977.

Tatia, Nathmal. *Studies in Jaina Philosophy*. Banaras: Jain Cultural Research Society, 1951.

———, trans. *That Which Is: The Tattvārtha Sūtra of Umāsvāti*. San Francisco: HarperCollins, 1994.

de la Vallee Poussin, Louis. "Le Bouddhisme et le Yoga de Patañjali." *Melanges Chinois et Bouddhiques* 5 (1936–1937): 232–42.

Venkatesananda, Swami, trans. *The Concise Yogavāsiṣṭha*. Albany: State University of New York Press, 1984.

Wagle, N. K., and Olle Qvarnstrom, eds. *Approaches to Jaina Studies: Philosophy, Logic, Rituals, and Symbols*. Toronto: University of Toronto Center for South Asian Studies, 1999.

White, David Gordon. *Tantra in Practice*. Princeton: Princeton University Press, 2000.

Williams, R. *Jaina Yoga: A Survey of the Medieval Śrāvakācāras*. Delhi: Motilal Banarsidass, 1963.

———. "Haribhadra." *Bulletin of the School of Oriental and African Studies, University of London* 28 (1965): 101–11.

Woodroffe, Sir John. *The Garland of Letters: Studies in the Mantra-Śāstra*. Pondicherry: Ganesh and Company, 1979.

Yogananda, Paramahansa. *Autobiography of a Yogi*. Los Angeles: Self-Realization Fellowship, 1977.

Index